passages

worship

- not very clear - reads like a sonnet

Riding
the Storm

- Poss. diss. idea - do re worship father + the son?

- uses phrases such as 'I think it is here... p42 + 'but I'm not sure' p43

Riding the Storm

A Guide to Radical, Spirit-Filled Worship for Worship Leaders, Musicians, Pastors and Creative Artists

John de Jong

Sovereign World

Sovereign World Ltd
PO Box 777
Tonbridge
Kent TN11 0ZS
England

ISBN 1 85240 362 4

The publishers aim to produce books which will help to extend and build
up the Kingdom of God. We do not necessarily agree with every view
expressed by the author, or with every interpretation of Scripture expressed.
We expect each reader to make his/her judgement in the light of their own
understanding of God's Word and in an attitude of Christian love and
fellowship.

Cover design by CCD, www.ccdgroup.co.uk
Typeset by CRB Associates, Reepham, Norfolk
Printed by Clays Ltd, St Ives plc

Contents

About the Author

John de Jong was born in England, but at the start of his musical career worked as a singer/songwriter in Europe. He holds a degree in Physics with Musical Acoustics and for many years was involved in professional audio while continuing to work as a performing musician, worship leader and acoustic guitar specialist. He has been leading worship now for some twenty-five years, most recently on the pastoral staff of the Manchester Vineyard where he heads up the music ministry and runs the Creative Worship Centre. He also has a degree in Humanities, having specialized in Philosophy and Religious Studies, and is currently developing worship-related courses as well as continuing his work as a performing and recording musician. John and his Dutch wife, Yelly, recently celebrated their 25th wedding anniversary and have three children, two of whom have now left home.

The Creative Worship Centre was founded in 1995 when John left industry to focus on ministry. Its aim is to encourage and equip creative people who have a passion for radical, Spirit-filled worship, and a regular programme of practical and inspirational events helps to achieve this. Many of these take place at a purpose-built training centre and recording studio just north of Manchester. In recent years the ministry has expanded into the Czech and Slovak Republics, and through the Creative Worship Centre Europe aims to establish a European centre to complement the growing programme of events, and to provide support and encouragement for European worship pioneers.

More information may be found at:

www.CreativeWorshipCentre.com

Author's Preface

Learning is a life-long process of osmosis. Over the years many people, knowingly or unknowingly, have mentored me. In some cases I've remembered who they are. In most cases I haven't, but like a good peppered steak, I've been marinated in a rich sauce. My early years in the Baptist and other conservative Evangelical denominations left a rich heritage in my life – the main stock, as it were, of the sauce. I was particularly influenced by Roger Forster when I studied for one year at Hildenborough Hall in Kent, on leaving school. He was always asking the question: 'Is it *reasonable* to believe?' He taught me never to take things for granted and to think things through. Only one year later, I found myself in Norway where an encounter with vibrant Pentecostalism changed my outlook forever. Since those days I've always tried to take the best of these seemingly opposite approaches to faith.

With apologies to those I've forgotten and find their work plagiarised here, I do need to mention a few names. During my time at Surrey University it was my privilege to attend Millmead Baptist Church where, at that time, David Pawson was the incumbent. His faithful teaching was inspiring. It was during those days that I spent much time with Kim Tan and others who were exploring communal living and being heavily influenced by Mennonite theology, particularly through the input of Alan Kreider. Another distinct flavour was added to the sauce.

It was not long after in 1986, that that I came across an unusual American called John Wimber. On meeting him for the first time, he said: 'John, I think we're going to become good friends.' It's quite possible that he said that to everyone he met, but it's true that I found him an inspiration. He was a remarkable man, and although we only spent a limited amount of time together, I was privileged to call him a friend. His teachings, particularly his profound and humorous one-liners, really got under my skin and as you'll see, they surface regularly here.

The Vineyard flavour was to become significant, as in 1989 I joined the Manchester Vineyard. I am particularly indebted to Martyn and Linda Smith, senior pastors of the church who, for the last fourteen years, have chosen to believe in me. As they have mentored me I have gained much practical wisdom, particularly in the application of theology and the dynamics of church structure and growth. My theology of worship was particularly influenced by Steve Robbins, a Vineyard theologian and pastor from the States, but I have yet to track down any of his work in writing. No doubt many Vineyard teachers will recognise elements of their work here and, in many ways, this underlines the effectiveness of teaching which is more than just theory: if anything, this is the greatest heritage of the Vineyard approach.

In the last ten years, through international travel that has included such diverse destinations as California and Siberia, the sauce has been enriched by exotic spices (as well as more mundane ingredients) which it seems, only grow in certain climates. Not least, I am indebted to the Czech and Slovak peoples who have taught me more about passion in worship than any conference I have ever attended.

My prayer as you read this book is that you will be inspired to express your love-affair with your Creator with increased passion and creativity, and that you will find here the tools to encourage others to do the same.

John de Jong
Manchester 2003

Introduction

I remember years ago being told by one pastor, 'Of course you realise there's no such role as "worship leader" in the Bible?' Well, I beg to differ. I was particularly struck by the story of Nehemiah's temple-building project that took place some two and a half thousand years ago. He was driven by a longing to see the temple restored to its former glory after years of neglect, but it wasn't until after he started the restoration process that some of the details came to light. While most people were out there on the building site with trowels and bricks, Ezra the Scribe, being a typical academic, was studying the finer details of the law. As he was doing this, he came across the instructions for an annual festival known as the Feast of Shelters. Realising that they had forgotten this major institution, Ezra came running out of his study and, before you know it, the workers had downed tools and were all partying!

It seems that Ezra's study was fruitful in other ways because Nehemiah's project was punctuated by frequent and timely reminders of the requirements of the Law. They wanted to get everything just right and in particular, we read of the reinstatement of the priestly orders – the Levites and the descendants of Aaron. The important role of worship leaders and musicians was not forgotten either, because:

> 'The custom of having choir directors to lead the choirs in hymns of praise and thanks to God began long ago in the days of David and Asaph.'
> (Nehemiah 12:46)

So I think it's safe to say that there have been worship leaders around for at least three thousand years.

I believe we are entering a time of radical restoration of the House of God – that God is restoring radical worship in His Church and that we as musicians, worship leaders and creative artists have a leading part to play. What I call 'radical worship' is characterised by:

- passionate engagement with the Holy Spirit using the whole person – body, mind and spirit,
- a renewed focus on the person and work of Jesus,
- an emphasis on scriptural foundations and principles,
- a synthesis of praise and adoration, prophecy and prayer,
- a renewed focus on the arts.

But most of all radical (of the root or roots; fundamental) worship is characterised by a re-examination or an awareness of the foundations – the roots of worship – resulting in practices which are not simply based on good ideas or traditions, but on a fresh understanding and experience of God's heart. Ezra's research was not just an academic exercise. It resulted in action.

Perhaps the question that I am most frequently asked is this: 'We want to improve the worship in our church but it's really hard. What do you suggest?' The word improve is often a euphemism for 'get rid of because we really can't cope any more', or, 'perform major surgery on'. It comes, more often than not, from a heart-cry for reality, life and relevance instead of dull religious routine. It's a bit like asking: 'How can we improve our town?'

More often than not people are looking for a quick fix, as if they could just get a quick service on the old car – maybe change the oil (always necessary), and a couple of tyres. But what is usually needed is a new engine and, once this is in place, you find that you need to deal with the corrosion that's eaten into the sub-frame. Before you know it, you've pretty much got a new car. Asking God for the oil of the Holy Spirit is not always a good thing. One thing will lead to another and before you know it your cherished car will be unrecognisable (to the relief of some and concern of others).

So how do we 'improve' worship? Well, bolt-on solutions don't work. You can't just start singing songs about intimacy and expect to be intimate. The surface of worship, like that of a town, is shaped over hundreds of years with roots that reach down into the deep subsoil of history, theology, sociology and ontology. Some roots need to be dug out and exposed for what they are – grafts from another plant. Others need to be nurtured and strengthened. Either way, some disruptive digging will be required and many churches are simply unwilling to pay the price. I hope that having picked up this book I can persuade you to become a radical workman (or workwoman).

So, some digging will be required I'm afraid. I've decided to do my best to become a good workman who *'correctly explains the word of truth'* (2 Timothy 2:15). How correct I am is up to you to judge. What I have tried to do is to be as rigorous as possible within the constraints of a book such as this, not shying away from some difficult subject areas and giving you many references so you can study more if you want to. But I am writing as a layman in many respects – I'm certainly no theologian – and my main aim is not to get too bogged down in unnecessary theory. Rather, I want this book to be a practical guide for those of you who, like myself, are involved in day-to-day work at the coal face – worship leaders, pastors, musicians, artists and of course, people who are 'just' worshippers.

My own role as a worship leader began in a Baptist church in Reading, England back in about 1970. In those days (I was sixteen then), the worship in the youth group could best be described as hymn bingo in that someone shouted out a number and we all joined in. It's been an interesting journey since then. For a while it was a literal journey, as I spent some four years working and travelling in mainland Europe as a singer/song-writer. It was a journey that started in Norway, where God graciously gave me a dynamic encounter with the Holy Spirit. Now, after many twists and turns in the road, I have ended up here in the Manchester Vineyard where I lead worship in the church and head up the Creative Worship Centre. Along the way I have worked with Christians from various streams and denominations. These have included Baptists, Methodists, Anglicans, Catholics, American and English Brethren, and so on. It has given me a respect for the many diverse ways in which we express our worship as Christians, but I have to be honest and say that I've also grown increasingly frustrated with the narrowness and intolerance that I see in many Christian groups.

I'm approaching this subject as a musician and I must confess to a bias towards musical worship, but I hope that we'll keep in mind that there are many other arts out there. We're getting excited in Manchester about using new forms of expression in our services: we are experimenting with visual arts like painting and video and exploring using our bodies more in dance and movement. I want to give you some concrete advice on how to lead people in musical worship, but please do keep in mind that there are other artistic expressions, some of which may be more relevant to our present culture.

I'd like you to read this book with an open mind. I've noticed that many of us do things in a certain way simply because 'it's always been done that way'. We've never stopped to examine the reasons *why*. I also notice an increasing frustration and boredom among Christians with the way we 'do church' and a corresponding increase in the gap between the church and our culture. If much of what *we* do borders on irrelevance for us as Christians, how much more is the Church an irrelevance for the society in which we live? As worship becomes more real for us as Christians I believe it will also begin to impact people around us. I hope, as we study this wonderful subject of worship together, that we'll take some steps, however small, towards a more dynamic and relevant expression of love and service for our Creator.

The concept of **Riding the Storm** has become, for us here in Manchester, a metaphor for exploring radical worship that transcends human limitations – worship which rises on eagle's wings, riding the thermals of the 'storm of the Lord'. That storms are with us cannot be questioned: the storm clouds of war that are gathering on the earth seem to reflect a heavenly preparation as God equips us for the coming season. It will be a season of great change as, *'the things on earth will be shaken, so that only eternal things will be left'* (Hebrews 12:27). Moreover, it seems likely that this shaking will challenge many of our accepted religious practices and beliefs. The question we want to ask is this: how can we engage in worship which rises above the storms that the enemy throws in our path? But more than this, how can we co-operate with God in the storm that He is bringing to reshape our landscape? The secret is to remain focused on God, to find the 'eye of the storm' where we are aware of God's presence and authority and where we rest in His peace.

I often say that teaching on worship is like doing marriage guidance classes. You can sit down with a couple and suggest maybe a romantic meal or two, or that maybe the husband should use a better deodorant, but at the end of the day how much they kiss is up to them. It's like leading the proverbial horse to water. So as we look at worship (and we'll spend quite a lot of time on theory as well as simple practicalities), don't forget that it's all about relationship. How much you *'kiss the Son'* (Psalm 2:12 NIV) is up to you.

Riding the storm

The wind is under my wings, I feel my body rising
As Spirit rain begins to fall
And dark against the sky, spanning the horizon
The brooding power of your storm

Deep in the thunder clouds the flickering of lightning
Sparks of fire in eagle eyes
My face against the wind, I'm eager for your coming
Your power hits my wings
I fly

And I'm riding the storm
I'm flying, soaring,
Riding the storm

The beat of angel wings thunder in the distance
The sound of battle fills the sky
The thermals of your love are spinning me higher and higher
I rise on eagle's wings
I fly

Chapter 1

The Search for Reality

'There are roads, and there are roads
And they call – can't you hear it?
Roads of the earth, and roads of the spirit
The best roads of all are the ones that aren't certain
One of those is where you'll find me till they drop
    the big curtain.'

(Bruce Cockburn)[1]

The journey begins

I love travelling.

The day I learned to ride a bike was a turning point in my life. From that day forward I was always wobbling off over the horizon as fast as my skinny little legs could carry me. I remember regularly phoning my poor mother from distant phone boxes to tell her where I was – not so much because I knew she was concerned for my welfare, but more because I wanted to share with her the excitement of arriving at a hitherto unknown and exotic destination, like Bracknell (then a small village five miles from where I lived).

The trend continued throughout my teenage years. I remember once starting out on a twenty-mile journey to the Downs and ending up in Wales, some two hundred miles away and, much to the horror of my longsuffering parents, it culminated in an attempt to hitch-hike from Norway to Australia (I was a budding hippie at the time and it was the thing to do). I still have itchy feet. Maybe that's why I now live only half an hour from Manchester Airport and have a job that regularly takes me away from home. And it's a good job because it combines my three passions – music, travel, and Jesus.

For me, worship is a journey into the unknown. How can a quest to discover an infinite, eternal God be anything *but* exciting? I am constantly amazed by God. He is never predictable, often incredible and always exciting. What's more, He has a quirky sense of humour and seems to enjoy (at times) being deliberately obtuse. I'm sure He won't mind me saying this, but sometimes He can be downright frustrating when He doesn't do things in the way that I'd planned.

So I want to take your hand and invite you to come on a journey with me. I'm not sure exactly what the destination will be because I know that there will be moments when I'll just have to point you in the right direction and leave you to your own devices. But I hope that while we're together it'll be fun.

Second best

As a musician I have had a good excuse to keep travelling. In recent years, the journey has taken me to much of Europe, Asia and America and has exposed me to all sorts of weird and wonderful people (on a bad day I think they're mostly weird). But one thing puzzles me and it concerns the amount of rubbish that Christians will put up with. How easily we are satisfied with second best, and how easily we slip into 'religious mode' or, as Paul puts it, *'confidence in human effort'* (Philippians 3:3).

I was leading worship once, for example, in a church in the north of England. It was a Baptist church with a wonderful atmosphere and at the end of the service my friend who had come with me to preach led us into a time of ministry. We'd brought a team of people from the Manchester Vineyard and all over the room people were being prayed for and responding to the great message that had been preached. I sensed God's presence (I'm more sensitive to this now than I was a few years ago), and could see people being drawn closer to Jesus in intimacy. You get the picture. Well, at that moment a woman dressed in black began to walk towards the front of the church, right down the centre aisle. She went up to my friend and said, 'We normally have the benediction now' and made it very clear that she wanted the service to be closed in this way. Being a visitor and not wishing to offend, my friend said a closing blessing: 'The Lord bless you and keep you, the Lord make His face to shine upon you, the Lord be gracious to you and give you His peace. Amen.' The effect to me was startling. It was as if a religious spirit had suddenly entered the room – I could almost smell it. People stopped praying and looked up. It was almost as if the Holy Spirit was saying: 'I've had enough of this – I'm out of here!' Ministry soon came to an end and people began to drift off home.

As we shall see in the next chapter, when externals become the focus, even 'Christian' worship can become idolatry. Worship can be like the conversation in a loveless marriage where the partners live in the same house, but where there is no real passion. Paul warns us against putting our confidence in human effort at the expense of real Spirit-filled relationship:

> *'For we who worship God in the Spirit are the only ones who are truly circumcised. We put no confidence in human effort. Instead, we boast about what Christ Jesus has done for us.'*
>
> (Philippians 3:3)

The search for God's glory

I know you're going to think me weird now, but when I was about ten or so I really loved reading the book of Ezekiel. I loved the strange language and bizarre images, and I suspect now that the Holy Spirit was using it to impart some prophetic gifting in me. I also read that passage in 2 Chronicles 5 where God's presence filled the temple like a cloud and I've often thought, 'Why can't we have more of that now?' My conservative Evangelical upbringing taught me that such longings are really fleshly and we walk by faith, not by sight, and so on. But always there was a cry in my heart of: 'There has to be more than this!' Don't you ever feel the same way? I sometimes wonder where the 'life in all its fullness' that Jesus promised really is. I've become convinced that the lack of what might be termed 'the revealed presence of God' is mostly due to a lack of expectancy on our part and a satisfaction with second-best. The marriage has gone stale, and it's not God's fault.

I believe though, that there's a wind of change blowing. In the last couple of years I've heard story after story of dramatic things happening during worship services. For example, in one church in Russia God suddenly announced in the middle of the service in Russian, 'I never change!'[2] The whole congregation heard it. I've also heard from two first-hand sources how God's presence came as a cloud during worship. In one instance of this, people could not see across the room because the presence of God was so thick. In another (which included sound effects which were caught on CD), the singer dived behind the drum kit tearing at her clothes because she thought she was on fire! I myself have experienced meetings where there seemed to be some kind of force field in front of the stage.

Those of us with an Evangelical upbringing might be concerned that such manifestations are at best a distraction and at worst demonic. We'll touch on this point later, but as a good friend of mine once pointed out, 'There's only one guest invited to this party.' It is right to question such manifestations: we can just as easily be sidetracked into false worship by dramatic episodes as by dry religious ritual. The key thing is that worship must be focused primarily on the person and work of Jesus. But I do think that there is real dynamic power when Spirit and truth come together – when a deep understanding of Scripture and tradition is combined with a humble spirit that embraces the things of the Spirit. It is then that faith really begins to fire on all four cylinders. If you would like to explore this theme further, I recommend Nathan and Wilson's book,[3] but right now let's consider the two smells of worship described in the Bible.

Formaldehyde

Think back to your school days. Do you remember what the biology lab used to smell like? I used to walk into ours and almost gag because it was so overpowering. The smell of mice and rats and various stuffed animals combined with strong whiffs of formaldehyde were, looking back, probably a distinct health hazard!

A health warning

I believe there should be a health hazard warning on a lot of our worship services for two reasons. Firstly, many that I've been to have had the smell of death and that can't be good for your health. I've walked into meetings and definitely caught a whiff of formaldehyde – the sense that something here is being preserved and there's no life in it. Like human death rites where we embalm and decorate the deceased to hide the awful truth, so also we have become adept at decorating and covering our services with a cosmetic veneer of religion so that maybe we don't have to face up to what's inside. I believe it's time to get real, to wake up and smell the coffee (or not, as the case may be!).

I'm being deliberately provocative here, but I think I'm in good company. Both Paul and Jesus referred to some pretty disgusting smells, and it seems that hypocritical worship is a stink in God's nostrils. Jesus obviously hadn't read that book *How to Win Friends and Influence People* when He laid into the Pharisees:

> *'Hypocrites! You are like whitewashed tombs – beautiful on the outside but filled on the inside with dead people's bones and all sorts of impurity.'* (Matthew 23:27)

And this is not the only biblical reference to hypocritical worship stinking to God. Time and time again God reminds the Israelites that He would rather have genuine mercy and compassion from them instead of mere empty rituals. It is clearly stated, *'The LORD is more pleased when we do what is just and right than when we give him sacrifices'* (Proverbs 21:3). Yet so often our emphasis is on offering a good sacrifice, having a 'good service', rather than on what is just and right. It may be right to let someone cry his or her eyes out in the Lord's presence, but we have been more concerned to keep the carpet clean. As John Wimber used to say: 'Our churches are like hospitals where no-one is allowed to bleed.' Constantly God reminds us in Scripture that He's looking for relationship with us, even if that costs us our dignity. He's also looking for integrity in our dealings with Him – for an honest and obedient (broken) heart. This was the issue when Samuel challenged Saul about offering sacrifices that God hadn't asked for:

> *'What is more pleasing to the LORD: your burnt offerings and sacrifices or your obedience to his voice? Obedience is far better than sacrifice. Listening to him is much better than offering the fat of rams.'* (1 Samuel 15:22)

These Old Testament principles are just as relevant to modern-day services as they were to the sacrificial rites of the ancient

Israelites. Paul, as you know, was an ex-Pharisee. Of all people, he could claim to have an excellent pedigree and education and today would probably have been addressed as 'the Rev. Dr Paul'. He could probably have put together a pretty cool service. And yet he says, *'I have discarded everything else, counting it all as garbage* [Gk. *excrement*]*, so that I may have Christ'* (Philippians 3:8).

I don't think we need to discuss further the smell that Paul was talking about. Personally, I want to run a mile from such worship. I'd much rather have worship that smells of roses. But, before we move on to nicer smells, I did say that there were two reasons why religious worship should carry a government health warning, and the second is this: empty, religious worship inoculates people against the real thing.

Vaccination

When you have a vaccination jab you are injected with a weakened version of the real virus. This gives your body the ability to develop antibodies without being exposed to the lethal virulence of healthy viruses. Paul warned Timothy to watch out for people that *'will act as if they are religious, but they will reject the power that could make them godly'* (2 Timothy 3:5). His advice was clear and unequivocal, *'You must stay away from people like that'* (2 Timothy 3:5). Why was Paul so adamant that Timothy should avoid any contact with such people? Well, it seems to me he was afraid that Timothy might catch something, that exposure to false religious practices would inoculate him against the real thing. He would have been injected with a version of Christianity that 'rejects power'.

You know the biggest reason why people don't want to become Christians? They look at us, the Church, and they say: 'If that's religion, they can keep it!' As I've already mentioned, if *we* struggle to cope with so many irrelevant and uninspired services, how much more will unbelievers be put off? In a recent survey commissioned by the Queen in her capacity as head of the Church of England to reveal religious attitudes in Britain, it was found that 65% of the population agreed with the statement that 'Jesus Christ was the Son of God', and yet only 1% attended church more frequently than once a month. In my view we need a radical re-think of how we 'do church' and we need to cry out to God for reality. Sally Morgenthaler puts it like this:

'In our infatuation with the cosmetic, perhaps we have forgotten that what will both draw and keep people is worship that is not only culturally relevant, but real. Real worship is a lot more than this week's production. It is where we allow the supernatural God of Scripture to show up and interact with the people in the pews.'[4]

By the way, it may seem as if I am criticising the established churches and embracing those who, on the surface at least, are 'radical'. This is not the case. I believe that many so-called 'radical' churches are just as religious and lifeless as the 'traditional' churches; they just express it in a noisier way. Moreover, it is often accompanied by a pride in 'how wonderful we are'. My observation is that God responds to a genuine cry of the heart and where penitent people are desperate, He will visit them in His compassion. I believe that the traditional churches hold the key to revival in many nations because many are desperately crying out to God.

Roses

'She anointed Jesus' feet with it and wiped his feet with her hair. And the house was filled with fragrance.' (John 12:3)

When we think of using the arts in worship, probably the last thing we think of is the art of the perfumer or aromatherapy, yet in both testaments the use of perfume is prominent. Pentecostals often talk about 'the anointing', and this is a reference to the perfume that was poured over the priest to dedicate him for service. We read about this in Exodus:

'Then the LORD said to Moses, collect choice spices – $12\frac{1}{2}$ pounds of pure myrrh, $6\frac{1}{4}$ pounds each of cinnamon and of sweet cane, $12\frac{1}{2}$ pounds of cassia, and one gallon of olive oil. Blend these ingredients into a holy anointing oil.' (Exodus 30:22–25)

The fragrance of this heady mixture must have been powerful, particularly when liberally poured (as it was) over Aaron and his sons to dedicate them for priestly service. They were soaked in the stuff! Everywhere they walked they must have carried the fragrance of worship. Everything they touched carried the lingering fragrance of heaven. There is so much we can learn from this passage, but for the moment understand that this costly, fragrant oil is symbolic of the Holy Spirit which, instead of being a restricted anointing for just a few priests, was to be poured out *'upon all people'* (Joel 2:28). Jesus went through Gethsemane on our behalf, and Gethsemane means 'wine press'. It was through Him being crushed, that the costly and fragrant oil of the Spirit could be released. The result is that, *'Our lives are a fragrance presented by Christ to God'* (2 Corinthians 2:15).

The perfume of Jesus

A couple of years ago I was at a worship meeting in the Czech Republic. We had just experienced an extraordinary time in God's presence, almost as if a blanket of holiness was pressing in on us. It was one of those meetings that I didn't want to end. I was leading the worship and had to get from the stage area to the bar to get some water (we were meeting in a hotel restaurant). I walked past a girl who was just resting in God's presence and I smelt a strong smell that was not unlike roses. It caught my attention because I had once smelt something similar at a meeting in Manchester. After the meeting I asked her: 'Are you wearing perfume?' She must have thought I was a bit odd, but answered that she wasn't. I was sure then that it was the perfume of Christ and later I shared with her what I had smelled and she was so blessed. The following year we had a large event called 'Catch the Fire' in Manchester with John and Carol Arnott. One day, as I was walking back to the venue with Mike, a friend of mine who helps me to lead worship in the Manchester Vineyard, we both distinctly caught a whiff of the same smell. It was amazing to smell it here, the perfume of Jesus out in the grubby Manchester streets. It gave me real hope that God is doing something in our city.

So this is what I want our worship to smell like. Not to reek of death and decay, but to smell of Jesus' after-shave. I want to be so close to Him that I can smell His perfume. A number of times since those occasions I have smelled this beautiful smell and it reminds me of when Paul describes the gift of the Philippians as *'a sweet-smelling sacrifice that is acceptable to God and pleases him'* (Philippians 4:18).

Worship in spirit

'But the time is coming and is already here when true worshipers will worship the Father in spirit and in truth. The Father is looking for anyone who will worship him that way. For God is Spirit, so those who worship him must worship in spirit and in truth.'

(John 4:23–24)

This somewhat enigmatic statement by Jesus underlines two issues which we must face if we want to experience the presence of God or lead others into His presence: the need for a genuine spiritual encounter and the need for integrity. We have to go beyond mere human effort that, as John says, *'accomplishes nothing'* (John 6:63). It is only through the work of the Holy Spirit in our lives that there is an eternal, supernatural dimension to our worship.

Escape from reality?

I would like to take just a moment to explore what this means in practice. I've seen people in worship going through contortions trying to 'connect' spiritually with God: screwing up their eyes in fervent concentration, agonising over whether or not the connection has gone dead, desperate for some indicator that the Holy Spirit is with them. Some even work themselves up into a trance-like state that behavioural psychologists characterise as dissociative behaviour – behaviour that is irrational and disconnected from reality in the sense that it is a departure from normal, wakeful consciousness. That the Holy Spirit does sometimes lead people to behave in bizarre fashions is not only possible, but also probable. Sometimes, when the Holy Spirit interacts with us, there is a mental and physical response that is abnormal – hardly surprising when you consider that you are interacting with a being described, among other things, as a *'consuming fire'*. Poke your fingers into a power socket and you would probably exhibit some form of 'dissociative behaviour'.

My concern is that there is much 'hype' about spirituality that is unbiblical, more rooted in secular philosophy than anything else. The Greeks, who have had an extraordinary influence on the way we look at ourselves, thought that the spirit was immortal and belonged to the gods, whereas by contrast the body was mortal and often considered degenerate. But God doesn't see you this way. The Bible always portrays people as whole people – body and spirit both equally important to God. It is why there is much emphasis in Scripture on the new body that God is going to give you at the resurrection, (you're not going to be wafting around as some disembodied soul). It is also why Jesus was so concerned to minister to the whole person. He placed as much importance on *'take up your bed and walk'* as on *'your sins are forgiven'*. Sometimes we forget that 'made in the image of God' means that we share the attributes of Jesus. Jesus still has a body!

Holistic worship

When we come to worship God we should not be so concerned to escape into some 'spiritual' dream-like state. Acceptable 'worship in spirit' simply means that we recognise there *is* a spiritual dimension to our worship. It is not to play down the role of our physical bodies and minds. Just as medical practitioners are realising the benefits of a holistic approach that recognises the need to treat the whole person (physical, mental and spiritual), so worship practitioners should realise that worship is not just a 'spiritual' exercise. This understanding frees us up to use our bodies in worship and to embrace many art forms that Christians often look down their noses at. God created us as physical–spiritual beings and it is when the whole person is engaged in Spirit-filled worship that we can be said to be worshipping in 'spirit and truth'. Jesus could not have made it any clearer: *'you must love the Lord your God with all your heart, all your soul, all your mind, and all your strength'* (Mark 12:30). The four Greek words used here cover every aspect of the human person. *Kardia* (heart) meant the centre of the physical being, including the seat of the affections and emotions; *psuche* (soul) meant the breath of life or spirit; *dianoia* (mind) meant the intellect and *ischus* (strength) meant ability, force or might. We have to love God with everything!

Maybe we think too much

I was attending an event in London once and found myself staying in a house belonging to a journalist who worked for a major British newspaper. We met late one evening and I described some of things I'd seen that day – people weeping, some being healed, extended worship times and so on. 'So,' he said, 'you're one of those happy-clappy types! It's a load of nonsense if you ask me. Put two thousand people in a room with some manipulative American and you can make them do anything! Trust me, it's nothing more than crowd hysteria.'

As I've already said, maybe some human responses are crowd-induced, but clearly some are not. My journalist friend's cynicism is typical of modern-day reactions to the things of the Spirit. If it can't be easily explained, treat it as irrational emotionalism. If it *can* be explained, give it a scientific name and assume God has nothing to do with it. This attitude presupposes that everything can be understood, dissected, measured, analysed or whatever. This is the kind of Western mind-set we've grown up with. And it's infected the Church.

A city without walls

I'd like us to look for a while at a passage from the book of Zechariah. Zechariah, as you may know, was a priest who had returned to Jerusalem to help rebuild the city (particularly the temple) after it had been war-damaged by the Babylonians. The date is around 400 BC. The Jews have been in exile for seventy years. The city is now overgrown and the advance party is surveying the damage and costing out the project. The book of Nehemiah tells the story. It's a very practical account of the rebuilding project. In contrast the book of Zechariah, who was one of Nehemiah's advisors, is very artistic and prophetic and gives us a lot of insight as to what was going on behind the scenes. In particular it gives us a glimpse of God's input to the situation in many pictorial prophetic images. Let's look at one of them:

> 'When I looked around me again, I saw a man with a measuring line in his hand. "Where are you going?" I asked. He replied, "I am going to measure Jerusalem, to see how wide and how long it is." Then the angel who was with me went to meet a second angel who was coming toward him. The other angel said, "Hurry, and say to that young man, 'Jerusalem will someday be so full of people that it won't have room enough for everyone! Many will live outside the city walls, with all their livestock – and yet they will be safe. For I, myself, will be a wall of fire around Jerusalem, says the LORD. And I will be the glory inside the city!'"' (Zechariah 2:1–5)

Measuring worship

Jerusalem (and in particular the temple) is symbolic of worship in the Bible and here we have a strange image of angels watching a surveyor at work. You could say he was measuring the place of worship. The angels then have an interesting conversation. One says to the other: 'It's pretty pointless doing that. Tell him he's wasting his time! The city will soon be so full that people will be camped all over the place – even outside the walls!'

A walled city, in biblical and medieval times, was a place of safety. At sundown the main gates would be locked and barred, and any unfortunate outsider would be at the mercy of the weather, thieves and wild animals. So much of our worship is like this. Barricaded behind our walls at sundown we sing songs of eventual rescue by the Lord of Hosts. The walls are not only physical, they are religious and psychological; walls which speak of our need to hide behind man-made structures, to be safe within familiar, predictable territory – hypnotic liturgy. Not only are we walled in this way, but also we like to measure worship with the same ruler we use for the rest of our rationalistic lives. 'Wasn't the service lovely! I thought the sermon was a bit long, didn't you? And that second song! Seemed to go on forever!'

Worship in the danger zone

The measuring line is certainly an evangelical weakness and, although we claim to use biblical rulers and plumb-lines, many of our standards come from secular thought and human insecurity. Soon worship is going to break free from man-made constraints and the old measuring standards will be useless. Worship is going to spill out into the danger zone. There is a call here to think beyond the familiar. It could be argued that the Church will not be salt and light until these walls are breached: until we take the risks that once again put us beyond human safety and into the arms of God. I challenge you to begin living and worshipping in the danger zone.

In search of the glory of God

This passage also talks of the multitudes that will get saved and be brought into the Church. If this happens it will be messy! We might as well take risks and get used to it now. Danny Daniels, one of the early Vineyard worship leaders, tells how he first got saved among the Jesus People in California in the seventies. He and many of his friends were ex-addicts who walked barefoot and – let's put it politely – did not have refined social skills. One of the churches that took them in was Calvary Chapel, run by pastor Chuck Smith. 'It was great!' says Danny, 'they had those little communion-cup holders on the back of the pews, and they were just the right size for your big toes! You could hook them in there and really get comfortable!' There were complaints from the regular church members that all these bare, greasy and grubby feet were soiling the carpet. You know what Chuck's response was? He took the carpet out. I wonder what it'll take for us to be willing to do the same?

The fire around and the glory within

There are two more key things we need to learn here. The first is this; that no matter how unsafe we feel, however much we go out on a limb, however vulnerable we choose to be, we have a promise from God: *'For I, myself, will be a wall of fire around Jerusalem, says the LORD'* (Zechariah 2:5). So in the distance, beyond the man-made boundaries, the fire of God is burning. You couldn't be in a safer place. Also, we see here the ultimate goal of worship: *'I will be the glory inside the city!'* (Zechariah 2:5). Surely this must be our heart's cry: to see God's glory once again in our churches?

Just after the events of September 11th 2001, I'm told that churches in America were packed with people trying to find meaning, reality and a context for what had just happened in their country. Now, a year or so later, those churches are emptying again. Why? Because instead of finding dynamic, passionate reality – the fire of the living God – most only found dull religious routines or skilfully put together religious shows. This is a serious wake-up call. We need to cry out once again for God's glory to be in the city. Every time we come to worship this should be our prayer. I long for the day when I can say, as the sons of Korah did back in David's time:

> *'We had heard of the city's glory,*
> *but now we have seen it ourselves –*
> *the city of the LORD Almighty.*
> *It is the city of our God.'*   (Psalm 48:8)

Offending the mind to reveal the heart

A couple of years ago, during an otherwise normal Sunday morning service, the Holy Spirit began to do some dental work on people in our congregation. During the week that followed, a total of twenty-four people reported that God had replaced their amalgam fillings with gold. A friend of mine noticed that one of his teeth was changing colour when he went to the bathroom during the service, so I had a good look in his mouth. I could see small light specks of what could have been gold all over a large filling. A week later, I peered into his mouth again, and now the filling was a pure white gold. It was extraordinary.

I noticed that some people I shared this story with were quite offended by the whole thing. 'Why didn't God just give them new teeth then?' was a common response, as if God didn't really know what He was doing. Others often just changed the subject. I found this strange because it was such a weird thing that my reaction was just the opposite. I wanted to investigate more and try to understand what on earth was going on: to ask more questions, to see whether things like this had happened before. Paul Cain once said that God offends the mind to reveal the heart. What I was seeing was people being offended because they couldn't get their heads round what was going on.

We should not be surprised at this. The fact that our heads are distinctly finite (some more finite than others!) means that it should come as no surprise that we don't understand an infinite universe or an eternal God. But perhaps more importantly, God has a history of being offensive. Biblical stories abound of God doing weird things with people. What about Saul, for example, who took all his clothes off and prophesied naked on the ground for twenty-four hours in the presence of Samuel (see 1 Samuel 19:24)? Or Elijah taunting the priests of Baal: when they failed to persuade Baal to light the bonfire that had been prepared on top of Mount Carmel, Elijah suggests, *'Perhaps he is deep in thought, or he is relieving himself'* (1 Kings 18:27). It kind of blows the theory that God is a perfect gentleman right out of the water.

The ultimate offence for many people is the cross. I think part of God's plan was to do something so radical to rescue us from sin that it would really make people sit up and think. For many, the reaction is: 'Surely God isn't *that* bloodthirsty, is He? Anyway, I don't see how someone being nailed to cross two thousand years ago could save my life.' Paul was fully aware of this and speaks about the offence of the cross (see Galatians 5:11). Rationally, it just doesn't make sense. As he says in Corinthians: *'I know very well how foolish the message of the cross sounds to those who are on the road to destruction'* (1 Corinthians 1:18). Later in his letter he explains why:

> *'But people who aren't Christians can't understand these truths from God's Spirit. It all sounds foolish to them because only those who have the Spirit can understand what the Spirit means.'*
>
> (1 Corinthians 2:14)

Once again, my challenge to you is to choose to believe God, even if it offends your mind. You will not be disappointed.

Truth in worship

We need to look a little closer for a moment at what Jesus meant by truthful worship. He talked about *'the Holy Spirit, who leads into all truth'* (John 14:17). It follows that real spiritual worship must by definition be truthful worship. Maybe that's why Jesus put the two together. Let's just remember here that to be spiritual does not mean to screw up your eyes and try and work yourself up into a 'spiritual state'. No, it simply means to choose to submit to God with all your being, body, mind and spirit.

John also says in his gospel that God's Word is truth (see John 17:17). The word *logos*, used here, is very rich in that it borrows from a Greek philosophical idea which used the term to describe the life force behind the universe (a bit like *Star Wars*). However, in John's writings it is used as a kind of code word to describe Jesus – that what was once just 'the force' is now a personal God revealed in Jesus. *Logos* also meant 'word': somebody's words in the form of teachings, writings, doctrines, or narratives. So, like the word 'worship' in English, as we shall see in the next chapter, it was a 'big' word. What we need to understand from this is that Jesus and His words must be central to worship. The Bible clearly plays an important part here. It seems to me that we need to get God's Word back into worship.

I've said that worship means to submit to God with *all* your being – body, mind and spirit. This perhaps highlights the most important aspect of truth. You see, Jesus was pretty scathing about half-hearted worshippers, people who pretended to worship but whose hearts were not in it. He invented the word 'hypocrite' to describe them. It literally means 'actor' and recalls Greek theatre where actors used masks in front of their faces in order to become a particular character. If you were playing Plato in the school play, you would get to wear the Plato mask. He hated pretence in worship. Isaiah put it like this:

> *'These people say they are mine. They honour me with their lips, but their hearts are far away. And their worship of me amounts to nothing more than human laws learned by rote.'* (Isaiah 29:13)

Real truth in worship, real integrity, means making sure that what appears on the outside is a genuine reflection of what's on the inside. The beginning of Psalm 24 illustrates this. David starts by asking a question:

> *'Who may ascend into the hill of the LORD?*
> *And who may stand in His holy place?'*   (Psalm 24:3 NASB)

In other words, 'Who's allowed to worship God?' The answer is:

> *'He who has clean hands and a pure heart,*
> *Who has not lifted up his soul to falsehood*
> *And has not sworn deceitfully.'*   (Psalm 24:4 NASB)

We need a quick lesson in Hebrew poetry. Instead of using rhymes like we do, the Hebrew poet would write couplets that meant the same thing. In other words, 'who may ascend into the hill of the Lord?' means exactly the same as 'who may stand in His holy place?' If you look at the first few verses of this psalm you'll see the pattern. In verse 4 we have two more couplets:

- *He who has clean hands*
- *And has not sworn deceitfully*

- *and a pure heart*
- *Who has not lifted up his soul to falsehood*

I've deliberately reversed the last two. Again, these couplets are simply two ways of saying the same thing, but you'll notice that the two on the left talk about external things (acting properly and not swearing), whilst the two on the right refer to internal things (right motives and genuine worship). David finds it impossible to distinguish between the internal and the external. This illustrates the Hebrew view of the makeup of man: that man is an integrated being, not made up of a separable body and soul as the Greeks later taught. As Steve Robbins puts it, worship involves aligning the inner and outer man. Ironically, quite a lot of our cultural hang-ups are due to the fact that there is a strong Greek influence in Western culture. We distrust our bodies and have inherited a Puritan distaste for them. Sadly, this has spilled over into a scorn for anything physical and has resulted in the undervaluing of the arts. *The Catholic Encyclopaedia* recognises this when it says:

> 'But it should not be purely interior worship, as Sabatier, with certain Protestants and most Deists,[5] maintains ... for man is not a pure spirit but composed of body and soul, and he should adore God not only in his soul but also in his body. This is the justification of all external manifestations of worship – genuflexion, prostration, kneeling, standing, the sign of the cross, the lifting-up or imposition of hands.'[6]

It appears that in this case Catholic theology is more biblical than its Protestant counterpart.

So much for theory, what about practice? I was raised in a church culture that was steeped in worship and yet when we sang hymns we stood there in ranks like 'onward Christian soldiers'. There was real heartfelt praise, but no movement. I guess I was a typical Englishman. It was when I was in Norway attending a wild music festival that I raised my hands for the first time. I felt an incredible sense of release and since that time, I've been slowly been getting physically freed up. The strange thing is that my inner man was always worshipping – I've always tried to make sure my heart was in the right place – and yet when I began to be more physical in worship it was like we'd moved up a gear. It felt like reality for the first time. This was reinforced recently when we had a visit in Manchester from Andy Au who runs an organisation called 'Movement in Worship'. He got us doing all sorts of strange things to develop our movement vocabulary (which is one of his phrases), including creating what he called a 'dynamic mass sculpture' which is an expressive, prophetic movement by a group of people working physically together. It was amazing fun, and again I felt a release in worship like I did in the early days. It is so freeing to be able to use your whole being to love God. When I get to heaven I'm going to be a very cool dancer with a body like Arnie (although thinking about it, that may be a bit over the top). Sadly, until then, God will have to cope with my ungainly flailing about.

So one cure for hypocrisy might be to bring your body into submission in worship. Many of us have genuine, loving hearts towards God, but find movement uncomfortable. Well, take a step at a time (no joke intended!). Raise your hands. Move in a way you've not moved before. Begin to rediscover the ability to love God with all your heart, all your soul, your entire mind and all your strength. And for those of us who sometimes go through the motions without the inner person being engaged, do what David did. Speak to your soul and say, 'Get your act together!' which is a rough paraphrase of Psalm 42:

> '*Why are you in despair, O my soul?*
> *And why have you become disturbed within me?*
> *Hope in God, for I shall again praise Him*
> *for the help of His presence.*' (Psalm 42:5 NASB)

Notes

1. Bruce Cockburn, *Child of the Wind* (taken from the album *Nothing but a Burning Light*, 1991).
2. Reported by June Richards from Kingsway Church in Sale. She heard this herself on a tape as the service was being recorded at the time.
3. Nathan and Wilson, *Empowered Evangelicals* (Servant Publications, Ann Arbor, Michigan, 1995).
4. Sally Morganthaler, *Worship Evangelism* (Zondervan, Michigan, 1995), p. 23.
5. A brief summary of Deism is given in the next section when we look at Conservative Evangelicalism.
6. Robert Broderick, *The Catholic Encyclopaedia* (STL, 1990).

Chapter 2

What Is Worship?

A quick tour of the theology and practice of worship

Before we go any further we need to define what we mean by 'worship'. Furthermore, the practice of worship that you or I are familiar with is the visible part of a much larger philosophical/ theological supporting root system that reaches down into history and tradition. Now, I did warn you in the Introduction (what do you mean, you didn't bother to read it?), that to be a *radical* workman means to do some digging occasionally. Here, I want to try and expose the roots of worship that reach down into the subsoil supplying nourishment. It's these that we need to explore to find out where the life (or disease) is coming from. Exposing the roots will give us a much clearer understanding of the plant we're dealing with. The main tap-root of worship goes down (or should go down) into biblical truth, so before we consider other supporting roots – like history and tradition – I want to look at some of the biblical roots of both worship and the antithesis of Christian worship – idolatry.

Worship is a big word

Worship in English is such a big word. We talk about a 'life of worship' in the same breath as a 'time of worship'. Think about this for a moment: if worship consumes the whole of life, how is it possible to stop and have a 'time of worship'? We also say things like: 'I worship the ground she walks on', or we talk about 'praise and worship' as if they were two different activities. We even call judges and mayors 'your worship'. When I was growing up I thought that 'worship' was the bit just before the sermon. So what does the word *worship* mean?

The Old English word 'weorthscipe' meant simply 'worthiness' or 'honour'. So worship means reverent love, respect or devotion (for anything), or it can mean specifically religious ceremonies or prayers. In this book we are particularly looking at corporate worship – how we express worth and honour to God as worshipping people together – but we must also look at the wider issues of personal lifestyle and service.

The heart of worship

The bottom line is that worship is all about *submission*. To give honour to someone (or something) means that you prefer them above yourself and praise them and also that you bow down to that person. In other words, you place yourself under that person's influence and protection and you submit to them. The focus of Christian worship is the Christ who revealed God to us. As Paul says:

> *'Christ is the visible image of the invisible God ... For God in all his fullness was pleased to live in Christ.'* (Colossians 1:15–19)

Submission is a key concept in worship because it reinforces the fact that to be a worshipper you can't be proud and rebellious. You have to recognise your own shortcomings, your own humanity and frailty, and bow down – submit – to God's supreme authority. In worship, we declare our dependence on God and the fact that even the breath in our bodies comes from Him. Submission is at the heart of the biblical concept of brokenness (you need to think of horses here, not pots), a theme that constantly surfaces in the book of Psalms, probably the greatest worship songbook of all time. The opposite of submission is rebellion, as illustrated by the idea of God having to use a bridle and bit to bring such rebellious people to heel (see 2 Kings 19:28 and Psalm 32:9).

Brief word study

Old Testament
There are two main Hebrew words which are translated as 'worship' in the Old Testament: *shachah*, which means 'bowing

or falling down, reverencing God' and *'abad*, which means 'serve'. The root of this word is same as that for 'slave or servant'. So already we see a link between the *devotional* side of worship that results in prostration before God and the *servile* side that results in a lifestyle of obedience. They are inseparable – two sides of the same coin:

> '*All kings will bow* (shachah) *before him,*
> *and all nations will serve* ('abad) *him.'*   (Psalm 72:11)

The idea of serving God was not seen a burden. Moses and Abraham, for example, are described as 'slaves of God' (*'abad Yahweh*), but this was a term of great honour bestowed on those that God had chosen (see for example Psalm 105:26–42). But even in the Old Testament, the motivation behind worship is love. The God of the Old Testament sometimes appears harsh and unforgiving and it seems as though fear, rather than love, is the driving force. Yet, as we look closely the loving heartbeat of God is only just below the surface. Even the giving of the law – which is inherently 'legalistic' – is softened by words of love. The scenes described in Deuteronomy when Moses is given the law are almost gothic in style: clouds, smoke, fire, fear, death and destruction. There is a darkness and gloom that sends shivers down your spine and yet as you read the clouds often part and shafts of sunlight suddenly dazzle you. We read, for example, that: '*the* LORD *chose your ancestors as the objects of his love ... He shows love to the foreigners living among you*' (Deuteronomy 10:15–18) and that the response to this revelation is, '*to love and worship* ('abad) *him with all your heart and soul*' (Deuteronomy 10:12). Even in the Old Testament love shines with startling power.

New Testament

The twin ideas of worship and service are carried over into the New Testament. Again, there are two key words that are often translated 'worship'. The first is *proskuneo* which literally means 'to kiss towards' and embodies the idea of bowing down in honour and adoration. It is probably derived from the Greek word *kuon* (dog) and carries the connotation of being like a dog licking the master's hand. This word is used three times by Jesus in this well-known verse:

> *'But the time is coming and is already here when true worshipers will worship the Father in spirit and in truth. The Father is looking for anyone who will worship him that way.'*   (John 4:23)

Some have used this word to justify a theology of 'kissing Jesus' in worship, in other words as a justification for the concept of intimacy with the Lord, but it seems that this is stretching the meaning somewhat. (Not that intimacy isn't justifiable on other grounds.)

The second Greek word is *latreuo*. This means 'to serve, or to do religious homage'. For example, in Hebrews 10:2 the word 'worshippers' could literally be translated 'the ones serving'. Another example is in Acts 24 where Paul, defending himself in Caesarea, says: *'But I admit that I follow the Way, which they call a sect. I worship (latreuo) the God of our ancestors . . .'* (Acts 24:14).

Jesus equated adoration and service when He used both of these words to counter the Devil's suggestion that He should bow down to him. He says: *'You must worship (proskuneo) the Lord your God; serve (latreuo) only him'* (Matthew 4:10). This underlines the old saying that 'you can't be good news on Sunday and bad news the rest of the week.' True worship does affect the way we live. It involves bowing down *and* it involves service. Anything that you worship will require you to sacrifice time, energy or money. In other words, you have to 'walk the talk'. Paul underlines this idea when he talks about worship in terms of a *'fragrant offering and sacrifice to God'*, yet equates this with living *'a life of love'*:

> *'Be imitators of God, therefore, as dearly loved children and live a life of love, just as Christ loved us and gave himself up for us as a fragrant offering and sacrifice to God.'*   (Ephesians 5:1–2 NIV)

The meaning of life, the universe and everything
In *The Hitch Hiker's Guide to the Galaxy* there was a computer called 'Deep Thought' that was asked to provide the answer to the meaning of 'life, the universe, and everything'. Its programmers were somewhat disappointed when they found out that the programme would take seven and a half million years to run. When Jesus was asked the same question, His answer was instantaneous: ' *"You must love the Lord your God with all your heart, all your soul, and all your mind." This is the first and greatest*

commandment' (Matthew 22:37–38). The questioner had asked: 'What is the greatest commandment in the Law?'

What you need to understand is that for a Jew, 'the Law' or 'the Law and the Prophets', really meant 'life, the universe and everything' because the Law and the Prophets symbolised the whole foundation of Jewish life and thought – the whole root system, if you like. Jesus' answer was that passionate and energetic love for God was the most important thing. It's a poignant reply when you consider that Jesus claimed to *be* God. What He's really saying is: 'The most important thing is that you and I have a love relationship.' We call this the 'Great Commandment', but Jesus didn't stop there. He went on to say: *'A second is equally important: "Love your neighbour as yourself." All the other commandments and all the demands of the prophets are based on these two commandments'* (Matthew 22:39–40).

So there are really two great commandments, and the second is *equally* important. What Jesus is saying here is: 'If you love Me, you'll love My kids.' As a father, I can relate to this: if someone does really nice things for my kids, it really blesses me. So this is yet another graphic illustration that worship has both a vertical dimension (adoration) and a horizontal dimension (service). This book is primarily about the corporate expression of the former, but I don't want you to forget that a lifestyle of service is just as important to Jesus as adoration.

The practice of worship in the Bible

The Bible is really a manual on how to worship and two key themes run through the whole text. The first relates to the big question: 'What must I do to be saved?' We cannot even approach God without some assurance that we won't get burned up in the process, for God is described as a *'consuming fire'* (Isaiah 33:14; Hebrews 12:29). The second theme is: 'Now that I am a child of God, how should I live my life?' Much of the New Testament answers this second question, but mostly in terms of moral behaviour. It's interesting that on balance there is not much advice on how to 'do church' in the New Testament, apart from some of the well-known passages written by Paul. I think this is partly because God wanted us to have to work out how to do things in our own cultural context. Even Paul's advice has to be interpreted with the local customs in mind: you can't just transplant first-century practices into the modern-day situation.

A second and related reason why we need to work out our own way of expressing worship is that any expression of love from one person to another will be unique to that person. Churches are no different: a genuine expression of love will be innovative and unique to that group, just as art reflects the style of a particular artist. I worry sometimes that worship teaching results in just replicating boring clones of someone else's ideas. I hope you will read this book with that in mind and be creative!

Some things are just taken as read

Another reason why there's not much practical advice in the New Testament is that many early Church practices were simply continuations of Jewish customs. The first Christians considered themselves Jews anyway (they just believed that the Messiah had come), and carried on worshipping in the way they'd always done. We read of synagogue and temple attendance, worship in homes, discussing current issues, corporate prayer and so on – life seems to be continuing pretty much as normal. The departure from the norm appears to be a resurgence of songs. It might not be obvious, but the New Testament is peppered with song lyrics that pop up often. As A.B. Macdonald notes, we shouldn't be surprised at this:

> 'A priori we should expect that a movement which released so much emotion, and loyalty, and enthusiasm would find its expression in Song.'[1]

Every move of God in history has resulted in new music and artistic creativity, and the birth of the Church was no exception! Examples of songs in the New Testament include Mary's song in Luke 1:46–55 (which is clearly based on an Old Testament model), and Ephesians 5:14 which runs: *'This is why it is said, "Awake, O sleeper, rise up from the dead, and Christ will give you light"'* (Ephesians 5:14). According to Ralph Martin[2] the Greek is quite rhythmical, and could be translated: 'Awake O sleeper, From thy grave arise, The light of Christ upon thee shines.'

It is quite clear though that believers in both the Old and New Testaments met together for worship, and it's useful to consider three settings – three sizes of meeting. This is summarised in the following table.

Festival/Celebration	Synagogue/ Congregation	Home/Cell Group
Inspiration	Identity	Intimacy
National (city-wide) event	Local community event	Family event
'In addition to the Sabbath, the LORD has established festivals, the holy occasions to be observed at the proper time each year.' (Leviticus 23:4)	*'It is the LORD's Sabbath day of complete rest, a holy day to assemble for worship. It must be observed wherever you live.'* (Leviticus 23:3) *'Jesus and his companions went to the town of Capernaum, and every Sabbath day he went into the synagogue and taught the people.'* (Mark 1:21)	*'They worshiped together at the Temple each day, met in homes for the Lord's Supper, and shared their meals with great joy and generosity.'* (Acts 2:46)

The festival or celebration

From Solomon's time onwards, the temple was the focus of religious life in Israel and the main venue for the big religious festivals. It was here that the nation would come together to express its identity and, at the time of Jesus, the population of the city would swell tenfold as four million pilgrims converged for the three big annual festivals. So many people came that during festival time the boundaries of the city were officially extended so that visitors could officially say 'we're staying in Jerusalem,' even though they were billeted in the surrounding villages. This is probably why Jesus stayed in Bethany when He came up for the Passover (see Mark 11:11–12). There were so many visitors for the Passover that priests had to offer sacrifices in three shifts, rather than the normal one, and the Kidron Brook, which acted as a sewer for the temple area, ran thick with blood.

When a Jewish family made the pilgrimage to Jerusalem it indelibly marked them as part of Israel – part of a wider community – and it reminds us of the modern equivalent that would be a city-wide or national event that attracts thousands of people. The leading of such a meeting – like a televised national event – would only be entrusted to someone (or a group) with a proven track record and national standing, and the focus primarily would be *inspiration*.

The synagogue or local congregation

Weekly meetings in the synagogue would obviously be more low-key with an emphasis on communal identity. No doubt the style differed from region to region and according to theological emphasis, much as churches today reflect the characteristics of the local community. Here, Christians can worship together with neighbours, friends (and enemies), and express themselves in their own unique way. Worship leading would be entrusted to those who are known in the fellowship and the main focus would be *identity*.

Family prayers or home group

The idea of a home group is nothing new. For a Jewish family, worship in the home would revolve around daily meals and special events, often encouraging participation from the youngest and the oldest members of the extended family. Family prayers became second nature to Jewish children. The earliest Christians simply carried on this tradition, seeing themselves as part of the family of Jesus. Our home groups are similar. Here, worship is led by anyone who can play a few chords (or press the 'play' button on a CD player), and the main focus is *intimacy*. As we shall see later, an understanding of these three settings helps us as we plan and lead worship.

A definition of worship

In order to be able to lead people in worship we need to ask three very important questions:

- What is worship?
- What does it look like?
- How do we lead people into it?

The last two questions will be answered as we go on, but maybe now is a good time to try and answer the first question and come up with a simple definition. We've looked at the various words that are translated 'worship' in the Bible and we've had a quick look at some Old and New Testament practices, so how about this for a definition:

▶ *Worship is the expression of a love-relationship with Jesus.*

I like this because it's simple, but also for the following reasons.

Jesus is the focus of worship
Firstly, it focuses on Jesus. As we'll see in the next section, it is very easy for the focus of worship to drift onto something or someone else. Certainly Paul was in no doubt about who should be at the centre of worship when he said:

> *'Because of this, God raised him up to the heights of heaven and gave him a name that is above every other name, so that at the name of Jesus every knee will bow, in heaven and on earth and under the earth, and every tongue will confess that Jesus Christ is Lord, to the glory of God the Father.'*   (Philippians 2:9–11)

It involves love
The second reason I like this definition is that it emphasises the importance of a love-relationship. It is so easy to fall into the trap of just doing religious things, forgetting that *who you know* is much more important than *what you do*. I'm often amazed at what people do in God's presence and what He seems to be able to cope with. On one hand we have very ordered, respectable 'devotions', but at the other extreme I've seen people flapping like beached fish on the floor, blowing Jesus kisses, crying like babies with snot hanging out of their noses and so on! Jesus seems to love it most when people get real and throw away their pride and preconceptions. How do I know this? Well, it's in crazy times like these I've noticed that people get dramatically healed, saved and delivered. God seems to like hanging around when His children get real with Him.

It involves expression
The third reason is that it involves expression. You can't just worship 'deep down in your heart'. Expression is a very broad term: we can express ourselves, as we have seen, in loving adoration as well as in loving service – in fact the two go together. I think it is in the film *Fiddler on the Roof* where the old Jewish granddad has a conversation with his elderly wife. It goes something like this:

> 'Do you love me?'
> 'I've borne you six children, haven't I?' she replies.

'Yes, but do you love me?'
'I've washed your clothes and tidied up after you for forty years!'

And the question is left hanging in the air. You know that they love each other, but what he is crying out for is a little more affirmation and romantic love. Jesus too, is crying out for His Church to get more passionate. In the past we've been pretty good at serving; now I believe God is calling us to a deeper expression of love and passion. Expression also speaks of artistic creativity and diversity. Let's not lose sight of that, even if we focus here on music as the main art form. We'll spend a good deal of time looking at creativity in Chapter 5.

Idolatry (false worship)

Sleeping with the enemy
In contrast, we could define idolatry as a consuming love-relationship with something or someone else *other* than Jesus: something that demands your attention (as love-relationships always do), your time, energy or money. Even the love of the *act* of worshipping can replace real worship: music, liturgy or art can all easily become idols. These days, idols are seldom carved out of wood and stone, but they are very common in our society. Steve Robbins, a Vineyard theologian from the States, talks about three things that can seduce us away from our relationship with Jesus: things, values or people. Let's look at them in a bit more detail.

Things
Materialism is the curse of modern society. I heard recently that 70% of the American economy is based on consumer spending financed by credit and that in the UK the 'average family' has a debt of £3000 – this figure excludes housing and mortgages. These are incredible figures. Our quest for 'things' has become an obsession and we will gladly get out the plastic to pay for our dreams. This may sound a bit stupid, but sometimes when I'm out shopping I see people about to hand over their credit cards for things which I know will be worthless in six months time and sometimes I want to scream out: 'Don't do it! It's a trap!' You

don't need me to tell you that things won't fulfil you, yet many people are trapped in a mind-set that believes they really will.

People

There are obvious cases where people idolise other people as in, say, the worship of Elvis, but some people-worship is less obvious. Dependent relationships develop which can become a primary life-focus and prevent people from fulfilling their goal to worship Jesus. Steve Robbins has developed this, but I'm not sure any books are available. He talks about 'the neighbour above you' as someone who you perceive as preventing you from reaching for higher goals in some way, an authority-figure with a negative influence: 'I can't do that because so-and-so won't let me.' Often the influence of such a person is more psychological than real because they have been mentally elevated to a false position of authority. Their influence and authority has become more important than the influence and authority of Jesus. The 'neighbour above you' has become an idol.

Ironically the relationship with 'the neighbour below you' – someone over whom *you* have influence – can equally develop into a consuming force which can prevent godly worship. In a sense you become a god in your own eyes. We don't have time to develop this further here, but it is clear that unless we bring our relationships to Jesus there is a danger they will become gods in our lives.

Values

As with many of the things we have discussed so far, they may be in themselves good, but when they dominate our lives and demand constant attention we know something is wrong. In fact, this is one easy way to expose potential idols: ask yourself, 'What do I think about most of the time?' Another way is to look at your bank statement and ask yourself: 'What do I spend my money on?' Jesus recognised this when He said, *'Wherever your treasure is, there your heart and thoughts will also be'* (Matthew 6:21). Now I don't want you to get paranoid! I recently bought a nice metallic red G&L Telecaster and I must confess that I spent a good few moments, if not days, thinking nice thoughts about it. (A Telecaster is a guitar, by the way, for you keyboard players out there – a *real* instrument.) No, the important thing is that we don't allow anything to develop into an obsession that Jesus is not happy with. This is why Paul told us to *'take captive every thought to make it obedient to Christ'* (2 Corinthians 10:5 NIV). Many Christians have obsessions which are entirely godly – the important thing is that Jesus must be Lord of our obsessions.

So what about values? Well, we all value certain things and build our lives around them – a large salary, some space in the morning, long-term friendships, education and so on. My wife and I, for example, value one of us being around when the kids come home from school. We feel it's important to be there for our children and that they shouldn't become 'latch key kids'. This value has meant that my wife is only able to do a part-time job. Values have practical outcomes. (We'll look at this later in the context of values that drive worship practices.)

Values, like things and people, can easily become obsessions. I know people who value a summer holiday in Greece so much ('it is our *right* to have an annual holiday') that they will sacrifice much to achieve their goal – mainly working all the hours that God gives so that they have enough money to blow it all in a two-week orgy of spending. This underlines a very important principle that *whatever* you worship will demand a sacrifice. The issue is not really whether you are going to worship, but rather what the object of your worship will be. We would do well to heed Paul's advice: *'So, my dear friends, flee from the worship of idols'* (1 Corinthians 10:14). We might think that Paul is referring to 'traditional' images of carved idols, but no – earlier in the passage he talks about it in terms of *'craving evil things'* (1 Corinthians 10:6). We're not just talking here about cosmetic life-style choices on the periphery of faith: there are life and death consequences:

> *'You can be sure that no immoral, impure, or greedy person will inherit the Kingdom of Christ and of God. For a greedy person is really an idolater who worships the things of this world.'*
>
> (Ephesians 5:5)

In love with Jesus

As seen, worship results from being in love with Jesus, so I'd like to explore what that really means. I'm sure you've known friends that have fallen in love. It can be nauseating: they spend hours gazing into each other's eyes, fondle each other in dark corners at parties, call each other stupid names and so on. Friends like these can be hard to handle at times. Wouldn't it be great if unbelievers started taking notice of us Christians because they saw such passionate love in us?

Irrational behaviour

When my sister starting going out with her then boyfriend (she was seventeen), she and I made a trip to our uncle's house in Holland one summer. We were due to be away from home for a few weeks. We'd not been there for long when her boyfriend turned up, having crossed the Channel and hitch-hiked through four countries to see her. (I didn't think she was *that* beautiful!) It goes without saying that he's now her husband. The fact is that when people are in love they are not *normal*. They do – as the 10CC song says – 'funny things'. Why is it, then, that we are so surprised (and worried) when Christians are not entirely rational? If current goings-on are a taste of things to come, then we're in for some interesting times!

Taking time

When people fall in love they don't have to be told to spend more time together – passion drives them to seek each other out. But it is true that to maintain a long-term relationship there has to be a conscious effort to invest quality time. So, we also need to slow down and take time to be with Jesus if we really want the relationship to develop – not just in our individual 'quiet times' but when we meet together for worship. We live in the kind of world where we're moving very swiftly from one experience to the next and sadly, much of our worship has been infected with this attitude. I believe one of the key things God is restoring to His Church in these last days is the ability to really know Him – to just rest in His arms, to hear the beat of His heart.

Contemplation

People in love enjoy gazing at each other with sickly expressions on their faces. Often, they don't seem to do much else! It seems almost pointless and yet we understand that the silent communion between two people reinforces the bond between them and illustrates the fact that much of our communication is non-verbal. I heard recently of a journalist who wanted to interview a Native American tribal elder. The elder agreed on the condition that they first spent some hours together looking into each other's faces. At the end of the time of mutual contemplation, the elder said: 'So, now you may ask your questions.' The journalist silently shook his head: he'd found out all that he needed to know.

I learned a similar lesson from a painting by Renoir. I had taken some time out to visit the Tate Gallery in London and, in typical tourist fashion, was rushing from one painting to the next without really looking at them. One, though, caught my eye. It was not a particularly colourful or striking work, but as I took time to meditate on it a poignant story unfolded. I began to appreciate the patient hours that the artist had put into his creation and I began to be drawn into the story. I noticed minute details that brought tears to my eyes and, by the time I turned away, I felt that I had actually met the young girl in the picture – she and I had become friends. How much more will we become friends with Jesus if we give Him a little of our time?

A warning

I don't know how you view casting demons out of people, working miracles and speaking prophetic words. For me, these are pretty dramatic things for a Christian to do – fairly impressive. On a scale of one to ten I'd put them pretty near the top. It is all the more shocking then to read Jesus' words in Matthew:

> *'On judgment day many will tell me, "Lord, Lord, we prophesied in your name and cast out demons in your name and performed many miracles in your name." But I will reply, "I never knew you. Go away; the things you did were unauthorised." '*
>
> (Matthew 7:22–23)

I believe we are entering a period of history when it will no longer be acceptable just to do things in the name of Jesus. It's time to work with Him in a way we've not known before – for us to know Him *and for Him to know us*. We can only be in this place of deep relationship if we are prepared to be vulnerable before Him and open ourselves completely to His Holy Spirit.

Delighting in the Lord's perfections

David talked about *'delighting in the LORD's perfections and meditating in his Temple'* (Psalm 27:4). However hard you gaze on God, you will never find a flaw. He is rightly described by James as the *'Father of the heavenly lights, who does not change like shifting shadows'* (James 1:17 NIV). For me, writing this book has been an illustration of that: I've been constantly amazed that the more I've discovered about God and His character, the more beauty I see. *Contemplation* leads to *adoration*.

We need to rediscover (particularly if like me you come from a Conservative Evangelical or Pentecostal background) the ability to delight in the Lord's perfections. Let me encourage you to slow down and take time to simply gaze at Jesus who was once described by Thomas Aquinas in the Middle Ages as 'the art of the omnipotent God'.

Notes
1. Quoted in Ralph P. Martin, *Worship in the Early Church* (Eerdmans, 1985), p. 40.
2. Ibid., p. 47.

Chapter 3

Firm Foundation or
Empty Tradition?

Why do we do what we do?

When my daughter Amy was little, she and I were cleaning our teeth together one day. She carefully squeezed the toothpaste onto her toothbrush and then solemnly banged her toothbrush twice on the edge of the sink before cleaning her teeth. I quizzed her: 'Why did you do that?'

'Because you do it,' came the reply.

Now it's true that when I was little I got into the habit of doing the same thing. You see, when I was growing up I would often squeeze toothpaste onto my brush only to drop it down the sink moments later because it wouldn't stay on the brush. I discovered that whacking it on the sink glued it securely to the bristles and hey, no problem! I'd almost forgotten I was still doing it. It's sad, but true. Anyway, Amy had no idea *why* I banged my toothbrush on the sink; she just thought it was the done thing.

Only a couple years ago, I visited a small group that was starting what they called a house church. It met – you've guessed it – in a house, in somebody's lounge. I couldn't believe my eyes when I saw what they'd done with the furniture. They'd carefully lined up the dining room chairs at the back of the room in two rows and then put the couch and armchairs in front. It was a miniature auditorium seating some ten or so people that turned up, all sitting in neat rows facing the front. The burning question on my mind was 'Why?'

Situations like this, although maybe not so obviously incongruous, are being played out every Sunday in churches around the world. I believe it's time to review our practices. I'm not anti-liturgy – some form of structure is necessary otherwise we'd slide into religious anarchic chaos – but why are we so quick to do things simply because they've always been done that way? Let's look at what colours our approach to 'doing church' in the twenty-first century.

Religious convictions and theological emphases

As I said at the beginning of this book, I've grown to love the whole Church and have worked with people from many different denominations. Many of my practices (as, I'm sure, yours too) borrow from different traditions. There's nothing new in this: even the Quakers in the last century borrowed practices from Catholic mysticism, even though they claimed to be at the other end of the doxological spectrum. In this section, though, I am going to be ruthless (maybe rude) and ask, 'Why *do* we bang our toothbrushes on the sink?' I'm going to caricature some of our cherished traditions. Please don't take it personally!

We'll take an extremely blunt pair of scissors, divide Christianity into three main streams and as this is a view of Western Christianity, I'm going to ignore Eastern Orthodoxy. The three streams are:

- Pentecostals and Charismatics
- Conservative Evangelicals
- High Churchmen and Catholics.

You must understand that I'm not writing as an expert, but as an observer: over the years in my musical work I've had to work with all three groups and these are just a few of the issues that have caught my attention. In each case, what we'll try and do is step back and take a cold, hard look at what goes on in worship, trying to understand strengths and weaknesses and best and worst practices. A key question we need to ask in each case is: 'What is the focus of worship?' As we saw earlier, religious practices can easily sneak in and knock Jesus out of the way and we can end up drifting towards religious idolatry.

Pentecostal and Charismatic practices

When I was nineteen or so I did a gig in the south of England. During the set I sang a version of the Leonard Cohen song *Sisters of Mercy*. Not the most edifying song in the world, perhaps

(Cohen's music was once described as 'music to top yourself to'), but nevertheless, I thought it was a pretty cool song. As I left the stage, I was surrounded by a group of concerned Pentecostals, horrified that I was unaware that there were demons inhabiting Cohen's songs and demanding to know whether I had been filled with the Spirit. They wanted to pray for me. Now me, I'm up for anything, so I was soon in the middle of a fervent scrum of enthusiastic tongue-speakers trying to pray the Spirit into me. I wasn't at all offended, but the prayers did go on for a long time and I didn't feel like much was happening. This was one of my first encounters with Pentecostals. It was a slightly unnerving experience but I appreciated their passion and concern.

Traditional Pentecostal groups (like Assemblies of God or Elim churches) trace their recent ancestry back to the Azusa Street revival of 1906, although many rightly argue that Spirit-filled Christians have always had a representation in historic Christianity since New Testament times.[1] They believe that speaking in tongues is evidence of being filled with the Spirit and have a strong theological emphasis on the place of Spiritual gifts, as did Paul in 1 Corinthians 12–14. They, like those in the Charismatic 'house church' movement of the eighties (who accept the gifts of the Spirit but often have less of an emphasis on tongues), view weird and wonderful things happening in worship as evidence of the Spirit's presence and tend to judge the success of a service according to how much sweat was generated. I remember once visiting a church with a keyboard player friend of mine and he came up to me after the service with beads of sweat rolling down his face, saying, 'Wasn't that a great!' I wasn't so sure, particularly since the preacher was convinced that a verse in Revelation – *'Nevertheless, I have this against you: You tolerate that woman Jezebel'* (Revelation 2:20 NIV) – referred to Margaret Thatcher!

There is, then, in Pentecostalism the danger of focusing too much on externals. *Activity* and *emotion* can become the centre of worship. Two further things result from this: the first is that worship, as is often the case, can be seen as merely a means to an end – in this instance it's to get something from God, to obtain blessing, healing or deliverance. Secondly, because activity and emotion are very human-centred, the worship can be focused on *self*. So the question, 'Was it a good service?' boils down to, 'What did *I* get out of it?'

There is another issue I've observed among Pentecostals and

Charismatics; that even in the most effervescent of services there is often an underlying conservatism. Practices that appear to be spontaneous and surprising are in fact predictable. The veneer of emotion or noisy behaviour hides a tradition that is as fixed as an Anglican liturgy.

Sometimes, I think the work of the Spirit is almost volcanic in that an eruption takes place, hot lava flows and big changes occur, but soon all we are left with is a rock stratum that has solidified into shape. On the surface we have the shape of molten rock, but really it's a cold crust. If you look at volcano you can see how its shape has been formed over the millennia and successive eruptions have added their contribution to the sculpture. The Church is like this too. Successive moves of the Spirit have forced aside old religious crusts. I guess we shouldn't be surprised when the pressure begins to build again. My own view is that we're due for the 'big one', possibly an explosion that will change the landscape forever. To change the analogy, I feel that the storm that is coming will bring judgement upon the house of God and many of our fossilised structures will be swept away by the winds of change. The challenge for us will be to work with God, rather than against Him. We need to learn how to ride the storm.

I feel like saying at this point: 'Some of my best friends are Pentecostals!' Well, I did say I would be rude and caricature people and so I've deliberately focused on extremes. I believe it's the case that the Pentecostal movement is the fastest growing stream in Christianity today, probably because they have so much passion and dedication and, crucially, are not afraid to 'let go and let God'. I believe God loves it when we forget our pride and do mad things for Him. I recently played at an AOG conference in Wales and, I have to say, that it was one of the most meaningful events I've been to for a long time (so I hope you Pentecostals will forgive me!). So let's move on and be rude about Conservative Evangelicals.

Conservative Evangelical practices
Ironically, the same chapter in 1 Corinthians where Paul talks about how to use tongues in worship (Chapter 14) is the same chapter that most Evangelicals get their mission statement from: *'But be sure that everything is done properly and in order'* (1 Corinthians 14:40). This was the maxim I grew up with and, instead of seeing weird things as possibly God's intervention, anything

which happened in our services which was out of the ordinary was considered at best an unfortunate interruption and, at worst, demonic. I remember being horrified during one service when the poor boy in front of me had an epileptic fit: I was disturbed that a demon could act like that in the middle of a service which only serves to underline the poverty of my world-view at the time. It's strange how so many Christians are happy to believe that the Devil can disrupt their daily lives and heckle during their services, while the Almighty God has His hands tied and watches impotently from a distance. My own view is that it is us that tie God's hands by our lack of faith, our desire to stay in control, our lack of expectancy and our satisfaction with second-best. As Frankie Schaeffer put it, we are addicted to mediocrity.

So here I'm caricaturing worst-case Conservative Evangelicalism, a tradition that rests heavily on the theological concept of transcendence and (it could be argued) borrows heavily from gnosticism, but a system that is also firmly committed to the Reformation emphases on the Word of God and salvation by grace through faith. Well, transcendence emphasises God's 'otherness'; the fact that He is far above the creation He made, it focuses on God's awesome power and majesty. Gnosticism was a philosophy that had some influence in New Testament times and beyond and it particularly emphasised a radical cosmic duality that rejected the things of the world and considered the body as a prison from which the soul longed to escape. Put these two together, and you get a world-view which sees God as pretty uninterested in the affairs of men, at least as far as the details of day-to-day life go. God is sometimes viewed as having created a 'wind up and let go' universe which is pursuing its inexorable course toward a pre-determined end. Calvinism, which ironically in its extreme form reflects Darwinian determinism, reinforces this picture by emphasising the sovereignty of God and denying that man has any say in determining his own future. These strands of thought also came together in an eighteenth-century philosophy called Deism which put great emphasis on the fact that God could be known through rational evidence, but denied any direct forms of revelation.

Conservative Evangelicalism is represented by most mainstream non-conformist denominations like Baptists, Methodists, Congregationalists and so on. Also, many 'low' Anglicans would describe themselves as Conservative Evangelicals.

So what does this mean in practice? The real strength of the evangelical corner is the emphasis on the Word of God. The Baptist church that I grew up in was typical in that it had a very ornate pulpit dominating the front of the building that was huge. Central at the front was a stand for the Bible. The architecture spoke volumes. A great strength here is the under-standing and exposition of God's Word. As I child I learned memory verses, took Scripture examinations and spent all of Sunday afternoon in a youth group Bible study (as well as attending morning and evening services). It gave me a fantastic foundation for my walk with Jesus. The downside is that too much emphasis was on theory and not on practice, and hence, a disconnection from real life. As John Wimber used to say, speaking of the Bible: 'It's the menu, not the meal.' So the danger for Conservative Evangelical worship is that the focus of worship can be the Bible itself, not the God who wrote it. Another practical result is that the emphasis on rationalism throws out anything that can't be explained (or pins the blame on the Devil), and at the extreme embraces a cessationist theology that teaches that spiritual gifts died out after the early Church period. This is impossible to justify historically or biblically, and is more a reaction to disappointment in present circumstances than clear thinking.

A typical service would be meticulously planned and executed, with a strong regard to themes – choosing hymns, for example, that tied in with the talk – and the pastor would do most of the work with congregational involvement being either pre-planned or discouraged. The second wrong focus could be described as *technique* and *control*. A good service would be evaluated in terms of how smoothly the plan was executed.

Once again I feel like saying: 'Some of my best friends are Conservative Evangelicals!' (In fact, most of my family are.) This one-sided and brief caricature highlights worst practice: when combined with an openness to the things of God (and strong teaching on the role of faith) Conservative Evangelicalism has much to offer, in particular rooting us firmly on the rock of Scripture.

High Church/Catholic practices

The Catholic Church, as an institution that has lasted for two millennia, has had an extraordinary influence on world affairs and culture. Regarded by adherents as the guardian of orthodoxy and by enemies as the great Babylon, the church claims a pedigree traceable back to the New Testament apostles. Clearly Protestants would not agree with the unique status claimed by Catholics, pointing out that Christians from other persuasions have always co-existed, some streams merging or breaking away from Catholicism, others flowing along an entirely different river bed. There are three things that we need to consider here which relate to worship, some of which we also find in Anglo-Catholicism (the Anglican 'High Church' whose practices lean towards Rome even though the church is officially Protestant). It goes without saying that, as with the other two streams we've considered, this is only a cursory glance at a huge subject. The three things are: prayers to, and veneration of the saints (including Mary), a high regard for the Mass which is the main focus in worship and a very structured liturgy presided over by a professional priest.

The main criticism levelled at the Catholic Church is that it does exactly what Paul warned us about: it has the form of religion but denies its power. It's so easy to go through the ritual without any heart engagement. The practice can be so easily tainted with surrounding paganism or secularism. Take, for example, Ireland where in country areas Catholicism sometimes has a very superstitious feel to it, or France (where I lived for some time) where people call themselves Catholics, occasionally embrace an outward show of church attendance and make the sign of the cross and so on, but whose lives are evidently based on secular philosophy and humanism.

Churches are no different than people: the greatest strength is always also the greatest weakness. The ability of the Catholic Church to welcome all people has become a great weakness as those on the fringes, some would argue, effectively practice a religion, which has little to do with accepted Christian orthodoxy. But the church's strength comes from the fact that where Protestants tend to argue and split, the Catholic Church lumbers on like some great combine harvester absorbing all in its path. We do not have time to develop this here, but we (Protestants), should not be too quick to throw stones: evangelical zeal or Pentecostal emotion can lead to a religion which is equally hypocritical or which slides towards what might be described as 'folk religion' – a religion which inadvertently takes on aspects of

the surrounding popular culture and beliefs. Also, because the
Catholic Church is such a huge organisation we must be careful
not to characterise the practices of the majority based on
observations of only a few. In countries like Slovakia, for
example, there are many Bible-believing Spirit-filled radical
Catholics determined to live their lives for Jesus and in America
one-fifth of all Catholics, about ten million people, call themselves Charismatic or Pentecostal.[2]

The second criticism concerns the worship of Mary, the saints
and the veneration of relics. Such 'idol worship' so incensed
Cromwell's 'holy army' that they spent much of their working
day destroying Catholic images and burning priests. Their legacy
is a Protestant distrust for all things artistic and a fear of holy
images. Calvin, for example, described the imagination as
'corrupted fantasy'. Any worship, as we have seen, which focuses
on things other than Jesus becomes idolatry. So is Conservative
Evangelical worship of the Bible so different? Or the desire of a
Pentecostal to enter a holy trance? Any practice taken to
extremes can knock Jesus off the throne.

My understanding is that Catholic theology clearly teaches
that worship is for God – Father, Son, and Holy Spirit – and for
Him alone.[3] Worship of the saints and Mary is not 'high
worship', but a veneration that looks beyond them to the worship of the Most High. It is a means to an end. The same is true
for the veneration of relics and holy places. The remains of a
saint are seen as evidence of God's grace in someone's life.
Symbols are places where the physical and metaphysical meet –
aids to help us visualise the invisible. The problem is that many
worshippers, unaware of the finer points of theology, are unable
to look beyond the symbols. We should learn two lessons from
this: firstly, it is easy for externals to take over, for the arts to
seduce us away from true worship. As we begin to be more
experimental in our worship we need to keep reminding ourselves of why we are doing it. Secondly, we need to acknowledge
that the Catholic understanding that worship cannot be just
internal but needs to be expressed physically is closer to the
Hebrew view of worship (and to Pentecostalism) than to, say,
Conservative Evangelicalism.

The issue we have not addressed is the role of the priest. The
danger with a priestly focus (or any kind of man-at-the-front
focus) is that he can be seen to be doing the worship on behalf

of the congregation, or that he is the only one qualified to be 'the minister'. Congregations can become passive and dependent on someone else, and those at the front can become addicted to the power of control. So whether it's a hot worship band, a gifted worship leader, a zealous pastor or a dedicated priest, the key thing is for those at the front to be able to get people to look beyond themselves and lead people into the presence of God.

Summary

The following table is a brief summary of the dangers in each stream we've discussed so far.

Charismatic/ Pentecostal	Conservative Evangelical	High Church/Catholic
Worship is a means to an end:	Worship is a means to an end:	Worship is the performance of a ritual:
A way to receive (healing, blessing, deliverance etc.)	A warm-up act for 'the word'.	All things must be done in the prescribed manner.
Substitute for real worship = *activity and emotion.*	Substitute for real worship = *'everything decent and in order'* (technique and control).	Substitute for real worship = *mysticism and superstition.*
Worship centred on *self.*	Worship centred on the *pulpit.*	Worship centred on *Mass* (priest).

The best of all worlds?

Having looked at extremes and worst-case practices, what can we learn that's positive from all this? Let's make another table (see next page) and try and identify the good things, the best practices, that each of these streams has to offer. Your list would be different from mine, but let's see how we get on.

No doubt you can think of other things. The challenge here is this: why can't we take the best from all these traditions? Just looking at this list you'll notice there's considerable overlapping: some things I've listed could pretty much be put in any of the three columns, so already there's maybe quite a bit of cross-fertilisation going on, although I think we need more.

Charismatic/ Pentecostal	Conservative Evangelical	High Church/Catholic
Passion.	Solid biblical foundation – not swayed by fads and fancies.	Sense of continuity and connection with saints of history.
Excellent Bible-based teaching.	Excellent teaching and apologetics.	Values external expression of worship.
Congregational involvement.	Engagement with intellectual and political world.	Values the arts in worship (especially visual arts).
Expectation that God will act through the power of the Holy Spirit.	Outward-looking focus (evangelical).	Not afraid of mystery. A deep reverence for the Passion of Christ as expressed in the Mass.
Willingness to be a 'fool for Christ'.	Heritage of great hymns combined with new musical styles.	Space for meditation and personal devotion.
Warm and friendly atmosphere.	Jesus-centred worship and theology.	Strong sense of worldwide community.
Culturally relevant music.	Real power when Word and Spirit are combined.	

Don't be too quick to throw stones

I suppose we need to ask: 'Why do we have so many Christian streams and then denominations within those streams?' Some division in the Church, it has to be said, is due to human stubbornness and pride. I know of a small village, for example, where there was a church split: about half the congregation decided they wanted to do things differently so they bought a plot of land opposite the old church and built a new place. On Sundays, the two congregations would walk to church down opposite sides of the same street, ignoring one another. Within about ten years the new church experienced another split, and before long this little village had three churches, three monuments to pride and stubbornness. Genetic flaws in churches always surface before too long.

But church division is not always negative. You could describe it as church multiplication (as we do with home groups in our church). If only one style of church existed how could we reach our neighbours for Jesus? Yes, streams develop because of theological differences, but I reckon style plays an equally important part. This is not to minimise passionately held theological or religious beliefs. Again, the greatest strength of 'religion' – that people are passionate about what they believe – is also its greatest weakness. People build their lives on what they passionately hold to be true so it's hardly surprising that they struggle with some-one who is equally passionate about the opposite.

So what am I saying? I don't believe in ecumenical unity that waters down beliefs until they are acceptable, but I would love to see more tolerance and a little more humility in the Church. If we see expressive diversity as a strength instead of a weakness, and begin to love one another, who can tell what an amazing impact it would have on our society? I believe this is the call on the Church in these last days.

Cultural backdrop

Culture affects the way we 'do church' as much as theology, perhaps more so. There are churches in both America and England for example, that would never use real wine for com-munion as alcohol is a cultural taboo, but this would be unheard of in France. Another example is the whole issue of dance and movement. Africans will happily use their whole bodies to express music, whereas conservative Brits are as stiff as starched shirt-collars. Let's look at some cultural issues relating to worship in England and see what we can learn, as well as highlighting maybe some things we need to un-learn. There's only space to look at a few examples.

Cultural conditioning
Let's take a look at a real hot potato: the role of women in worship. You must have noticed the impact of feminism on our culture. Political correctness demands that we refer to the 'chair person' or 'chair' as opposed to 'chairman'. Liberal Christian feminists insist on calling God 'she'. Does this affect our approach as to whom can be involved in worship, and should it? It would be stupid for me to try and look at this huge subject in just a few lines, but let me give you a few things to get you thinking. First of all I believe we need to go back to the Bible for guidance – that our church culture should be driven primarily by biblical principles. Having said that, the Bible is strangely silent about many of the practical issues surrounding church practice; I think, as has already been noted, that this is because God has

given us a certain amount of creative freedom. If *'every tribe and language and people and nation'* (Revelation 5:9) is to be represented before the throne of God, there has to be space for a significant amount of cultural diversity. Now, many Christians will quote Paul on this subject of women in leadership:

> *'Women should be silent during the church meetings. It is not proper for them to speak. They should be submissive, just as the law says. If they have any questions to ask, let them ask their husbands at home, for it is improper for women to speak in church meetings.'*   (1 Corinthians 14:34–35)

But it's not quite as simple as this. We do not have the right to transplant first-century concepts into the twenty-first century otherwise we would have to, for example, accept slavery as an acceptable practice. As Dr N.H. Creegan (who describes herself as a low Anglican) notes:

> 'But I think there is ample evidence that we are on shaky ground when we exclude women [from leadership in the church], even without detailed analyses of these particular few verses – 1 Tim and 1 Corinthians.'[4]

And what about the current involvement of women in the Church? My own aunt was a wonderful lady who was the driving force behind a mission in Reading in the mid-1900s that has since been established as a thriving church. Every time I pass the sign to that church I think of her faithful leadership. What if she, and the thousands of women like her currently achieving extraordinary things for God, had been excluded from ministry? Where would that leave the Church today? Such questions need genuine answers.

Consider also the attitude of Jesus to the women around Him. He had disciples that were women (unheard of for a respectable rabbi), financial supporters that were women, chosen witnesses to the resurrection were also women, and so on. And this in a society where a daily male prayer was: 'blessed be God that hath not made me a woman', and where Pharisees prayed: 'I thank you God that I was not made a dog or a woman', and where women were not allowed to be witnesses in court. He overturned completely the patriarchal emphasis and social norms of the day.[5] Some have argued that the reinstatement of male dominance occurred in the second or third centuries, whereas the intention of Jesus was always that women should co-lead with men.

What I've noticed myself, certainly as far as worship teams go, is that the girls are often denied leadership training or are just expected to be 'backing singers', backing up the men. In other contexts, I've noticed that whilst women are allowed to lead in some measure, there's an undercurrent of condescension, as if the situation is perhaps only second best.

Oral law

This situation is an example of a modern 'oral law'. By the time that Jesus walked the earth the Torah, the books of the Law that are the first five books of our Bible, was supplemented by a commentary of 'oral law' known as the *Midrash*. This was a commentary that the scribes (the academics of the day) committed to memory and developed by adding their own sayings and footnotes. These then formed the basis of another commentary called the *Mishnah* that, with the Midrash, formed the basis of yet a third book of oral law called the *Talmud*. It was this collection of oral law that Jesus often scorned as 'your traditions'.[6] My worry is that we have many modern-day equivalents of oral traditions. Many may have some scriptural basis, but many more are distortions of the truth. 'Women should not be in charge of worship' is one example. You need to decide for yourself whether this is true.

Two more short examples to get you thinking. Ask yourself: 'What does the architecture and set up of our church communicate about what we believe?' If you all face the front, why do you do this? Does the worship leader always stand in the centre of the stage? Why? Is there some kind of oral law that says 'the congregation must face the stage'? Why not put the worship team in the middle of the room with the congregation all round? Finally, why do most Conservative Evangelical or Pentecostal services start with 'a time of worship' followed by 'the word'? If worship is primarily a response to the revealed presence of God, wouldn't it be better the other way round?

Donald Craybill gets straight to the heart of the issue when he says:

> 'The values, beliefs, and norms of our society become so deeply engrained within our thought processes that it's

difficult to conceive of acting a different way. The way of Jesus often appears upside-down or backwards in contrast to the prevailing value system which our minds have absorbed so thoroughly. If it does anything, the Kingdom of God shatters most of the assumptions which govern our social life. As Kingdom citizens we don't just assume that things are right just because "that's the way they are".[7]

I challenge you to question your religious assumptions with the same vigour that you would question secular practices around you.

Cultural relevance

Church and culture is an interesting subject. On the one hand we are *in* the world, yet Jesus warns us not to be *of* the world. We need to build bridges with the culture around us without losing our ability to be what Jesus called salt and light. I'd like to put it like this: we need to be culturally relevant but not culturally driven. The way we become relevant is not by simply mimicking the world around us, but by communicating and engaging with our culture in terms that it understands. Here I think we can use our caricatures of the three 'streams' of Western Christianity to teach us a lesson. The most important thing, in my view, is the need for reality and power. Here we need to take a lesson from the Pentecostals. We live in a post-modern culture: this means that people don't think as rationally as they used to; they don't think linearly. People aren't persuaded by arguments in the same way that they used to be, they say, 'Well, that's great for you, but I don't believe it.' Truth is no longer what Schaeffer called 'true truth' – absolute truth; everything is relative. What people need in a society like this is for us to walk in power. Once word gets round that God is healing AIDS in the church, or people twisted with congenital defects are being straightened out, then people will be queuing up to get in. But we do need words, and here we can learn from the Evangelicals in particular. Ideas have great power (which is why I wanted to get these thoughts down on paper). Ideas have children, and demonic ideas are no exception. Philosophies straight from the pit of hell are dragging people back to their source. People are literally dying because some academic, living a life of luxury in a leafy suburb, decides to put his hell-inspired ideas down on paper. So, we need to engage with the political and social debates of our day and we need to pray for those apologists that are working on our behalf. Thirdly, we need to learn from the High Church and Catholic traditions. Post-modernism, instead of being seen as a threat, is in fact a wonderful opportunity for the Church to engage with culture. It is a culture which is rediscovering the value of symbols and stories. It is also much more visual than it has ever been. Christian story and symbol can speak volumes where words fail, and a meditative space in a world so full of noise would help many people discover the reality of the presence of God.

So how might this affect our worship services? I would suggest that Church in twenty years time will be unrecognisable. Here are some radical ideas: begin to become more visual and space-orientated in your approach to worship. Is it really necessary to have rows of people facing the front? Why not have a worship time where different groups of people are simultaneously engaged in different aspects of worship in different areas of your room or building, perhaps only coming together briefly for a corporate act? Use more of the arts in worship, particularly visual and plastic arts which prophetically speak of the things of God. Rediscover the sense of a 'holy place'. Set aside a room for worship. Dedicate it to God and encourage worship to go on twenty-four hours a day, seven days a week. Invite people from the streets to see it as an oasis to escape from the treadmill of normality. Pray God's blessings on them and for the healing of their physical and emotional hurts. Don't view the church as bounded by four walls. Think of it more as the yeast in the dough. This means you'll need to take a more active role in encouraging those artists, apologists and musicians who see their calling as being out there on the streets or in the debating chambers. It also means more support for those of us who have 'normal' work. Teach people how to worship in the workplace. But let me remind you that:

> '. . . *whatever you do or say, let it be as a representative of the Lord Jesus, all the while giving thanks through him to God the Father.'*   (Colossians 3:17)

In all our experimentation and artistic creativity, let's determine to keep *'our eyes on Jesus, on whom our faith depends from start to finish'* (Hebrews 12:2). We face enormous challenges here at the birth of a new millennium. The storm clouds are gathering on the earth and we desperately need to cry out for God to empower us for the coming season. It doesn't matter how artistic or culturally relevant our services are: only the powerful presence of God will demonstrate to a lost world that God is real. We must no longer be satisfied with second best.

Driving culture

My wife and I and some friends rented a narrow boat once and went on a holiday on the Grand Union Canal. Narrow boats are, maybe not surprisingly, narrow, but they are also very heavy like long residential barges. We were pottering along at the usual four or so knots one day with my wife (a complete novice) at the helm, when we heard her cry for help. We were on a wide section of the canal with houseboats moored alongside the bank and when I came up from the cabin below I saw that we were heading, slowly and inevitably, on a collision course with one of the houseboats. The fact that it was all happening in slow motion made it really excruciating and I had visions of the bow of our boat splintering into someone's lounge. All I could do was pull the tiller in the opposite direction (my poor wife had got confused), increase power to the engine and wait. Our trajectory, which had been a ponderous arc towards the centre of the moored boat, slowly began to change direction. It was one of those genuinely heart-stopping, hold-your-breath moments that seemed to last forever. Our course slowly changed, yet we were still heading towards the bank. By some miracle (probably angels pushing us sideways!) we succeeded in passing the moored boat with literally just one inch of clearance and headed back out into clear water. I breathed out finally, my heart racing like my old Honda 500.

Cultural change takes time

Later, God spoke to me through this. He showed me that churches are often narrow, with blinkered vision and limited practice. At the same time they are heavy. Some, like the houseboat, are firmly tied to old traditional moorings probably related to old blessings. Some are moving, but progress is slow and often headed in the wrong direction. He showed me that we need to do two things. We need to increase the power, and we need to push the tiller over. The power analogy is obvious, but what about the tiller? The tiller is the lever that connects to the rudder of the boat, and the rudder is the place where (to mix analogies) the rubber hits the road. It's where turbulence is created in the water, where pressure is created which eventually causes the whole boat to change course. Leadership is the ability to apply pressure at the right time and in the right place – you can only do this by looking ahead of you – by having a long-term perspective on where you want to go. Pressure points are created when we begin to change our practices; these cause turbulence and friction which is caused by a departure from the normal course, yet without such disruption change is impossible.

The problem is that churches are full of people who are quite comfortable, people who are culturally conditioned to the status quo, who never question the need for change. I believe that God has given prophets and creative people to the Church in order to create turbulence at times. To make us aware that there is cultural water around us and maybe we are just drifting with the flow. Prophetic leadership is needed that can harness the power of turbulence, and we need an understanding that cultural changes do take time, but if we keep our eye on the trajectory we'll get there in the end.

Stay connected

The tiller is a crucial part in the control chain. I was out sailing once in a brisk wind when the tiller came out of its socket. The result was a capsize. The tiller represents the connection between the prophets (often creative, artistic people) and the leaders. It's only when there's a healthy working relationship between the two that the boat makes headway. Disconnection results in disaster. Many of the historical capsizes that we read about are a result of dysfunctional leadership, or a breakdown in the relationship between leaders and prophets. Think, for example of the turbulent relationship Samuel had with Saul which often led to harsh words being spoken (see for example 1 Samuel 15), or of the number of churches where there is open warfare going on between vicar and organist. Sometimes it's the fault of the creative, prophetic people who resist being under authority. Sometimes it's the fault of the leaders who, finding prophetic people a pain in the neck, wash their hands of them. Staying connected is the key to functioning correctly.

Heading for open sea

Returning briefly to the subject of power. Narrow boats are generally powered by old Perkins diesel engines (the same engines that used to power trucks in the old days). Technology has moved on since the 1950s. What would stop us dropping a turbo-diesel cruiser engine into a narrow boat? The main problem would be that we would break local laws. On inland waterways in Britain the speed limit is normally about five knots and, even where there is no speed limit, courtesy demands that you keep your speed down so as not to annoy the neighbours. Need I say more? I don't think we were designed to just potter about on man-made waterways – to be constantly mindful of human restrictions, fearful of annoying the neighbours. It's time that the Church headed for the freedom of the open sea. Let's stop worrying about how much wash we make; it's time to make waves!

Here's a quick postscript on engines. John Paul Jackson tells the story of a Canadian who found a bargain boat in a scrap yard. Unaware that it was full of dry rot, he asked a local boat yard to put a powerful new engine in. Proudly cruising on the lake during the maiden voyage he had to slow down in a hurry. He threw the drive into reverse and increased power with the result that the engine splintered out of the back of the boat, plunging to the bottom of the lake. The boat itself was only saved because it was close to a jetty. The moral is this: check for dry rot before you increase the power. We'll learn how to do this in the next chapter.

Who's in the driving seat?

Historically the Church used to drive culture. Artists, musicians and writers found refuge and support in the Church. The Church was known as a patron of the arts. Musicians such as J.S. Bach recognised that their gifts were God-given; on all his manuscripts Bach added the footnote 'Deo Gloria' ('to the glory of God'). Even Descartes, bless him, having written 'I think, therefore I am', went down to his local Catholic church to thank God for this amazing discovery.

In the 1850s though, the Church found itself under attack. Rationalism was sweeping Europe, Darwin was publishing *Origin of Species*, and the truth of the Bible itself was under attack from a liberal theology coming across the channel from Germany. On top of this, the Church had been labouring away for years to try and bring about social reform and had begun to make big inroads into politics and government. Ironically, success here resulted in more problems: now that secular society had a social conscience it took over the role of the Church – the Church found its services even less in demand. The result was entrenchment. The Church dug in behind 'enemy' lines, engaging less and less with popular culture. They began to sing songs which borrowed themes from the American Civil War – songs which spoke of 'holding the fort' until Jesus came to the rescue.[8]

Residues of this mind-set permeate much of our current thinking and yet society has moved on. The truth of science is no longer such an absolute. Quantum mechanics and the theory of relativity (and, more recently, chaos theory) have challenged the comfortable certainties of Newtonian physics, and people are beginning to question things again. Against this backdrop of uncertainty, many are searching for meaning in their lives and are rediscovering spirituality. We have a unique opportunity here at the beginning of this millennium to lead those who are searching towards the truth of the Good News. My own view is that in the next ten years or so we are going to see significant deterioration in our society as we experience moral meltdown, lawlessness and panic. As a church, we are called to be a refuge from the storm – not to assimilate the negative aspects of the culture around us, but to become a strong light shining in the darkness, which will lead many to find salvation.

Notes

1. See, for example, E.H. Broadbent, *The Pilgrim Church* (Pickering and Inglis, 1985, first published in 1931). Also, Kim Tan, *Lost Heritage* (Highland Books, Surrey, 1996).
2. Naisbitt and Aburdene, *Megatrends 2000* (Avon Books New York, 1990), p. 311.
3. See, for example, 'Worship' in *The Catholic Encyclopaedia*.
4. N.C. Creegan, *Feminism and the Bible* (Bible College of New Zealand, www.vuw.ac.nz).
5. See Donald B. Craybill, *The Upside-Down Kingdom* (Marshall Morgan and Scott, 1985), pp. 238–246.
6. See, for example, Mark 7:9.
7. Donald B. Craybill, *The Upside-Down Kingdom* (Marshall Morgan and Scott, 1985), p. 28.
8. 'Hold the Fort' is number one in Sankey's *Sacred Songs and Solos*, published in the 1860s. The chorus goes: 'Hold the fort for I am coming, Jesus signals still; wave the answer back to heaven, by Thy Grace we will!'

Chapter 4

Managing Change

How to evaluate your worship practices and develop skills that will enable you to successfully introduce change

Change is here to stay

'There's one thing you can be sure of,' so the saying goes, 'change is here to stay.' The management – or maybe I should say leadership – of change must therefore be a key skill: a skill that we desperately need to learn. Instead of being 'blown about by every wind of doctrine' – every new fad that comes along – we need to learn how to steer a course towards the open sea without being sidetracked into stagnant backwaters or fatal rapids. Martyn Smith, the senior pastor of the Manchester Vineyard, puts it this way: 'Change brings challenge; challenge means staying closer to God; closeness to God brings life; life means growth; and growth means change.' And so the cycle of change and growth continues. The Church is an organism, not an organisation, and organisms grow or they die.

As seen, the culture around us is developing; history is unfolding, and the pace of change is phenomenal. On the surface of our society waves of new technology continuously wash over us (who could have foreseen the meteoric rise of internet use?) while underneath, the moral foundations are shifting and seething like undercurrents that eat at the shoreline. The political, cultural and sociological landscape is changing shape at a breathtaking rate. The storm clouds are on the horizon and already we hear distant rumbles of thunder.

A paradox is that the average person on the street is bored. She goes to work each day, taking the same route; she sits at the same desk in front of the same computer, the same telephone; talks to the same people at lunchtime; dreams of the weekend where she visits the same health club. And each night she wearily makes her way upstairs to the same bed. The anaesthetic routine dulls her mind. She seldom thinks of next year, let alone her eternal destiny.

> *'Satan, the god of this evil world, has blinded the minds of those who don't believe, so they are unable to see the glorious light of the Good News that is shining upon them.'*   (2 Corinthians 4:4)

Psychologists say that our make-up is not suited to the static life, that our hunter-gatherer instincts make us nomads by nature. What they don't understand is that we were designed for worship, and worship is not a static experience, it's a journey. Moreover, we don't have to wait until we get to heaven for the adventure to begin. Michael Mayne, sometime Dean of Westminster, puts it like this:

> 'If spirituality means the way we grow into the kind of being that we are intended to be, then the starting point is not a striving after another world, but a deepening awareness of the true nature of this world, and our place within it.'[1]

The parody of worship put out by the enemy's propaganda machine – that worship is sitting on a white cloud doing nothing for eternity – is a ploy to distract people from the reality that worship is an adventure. If the exploration of the Amazon basin is such a draw for the adventurous, how much more is the journey towards an infinite God who is about to create a new heaven and a new earth?

> *'That is what the Scriptures mean when they say:*
>   *"No eye has seen, no ear has heard,*
>   *and no mind has imagined*
>   *what God has prepared*
>   *for those who love him."'*   (1 Corinthians 2:9)

Being captain of the Starship Enterprise would seem boring in comparison! Worship is a magical journey, a developing relationship with an eternal God who is full of surprises. We see this clearly modelled in the Old Testament, and I'd like to focus on this briefly.

Time to move on

The Old Testament is the story of a journey. The first steps of the journey are tragic and lonely as Adam and Eve are expelled from the Garden in disgrace. But God is never far away, and soon we see Him stooping down to earth again to meet with Noah and Abraham, and the journey continues with God coaxing His people towards relationship. A nation grows from the faith of Abraham and soon a whole nation, rescued from slavery, is being shepherded across a desert by a jealous, protective God. The narrative often zooms in on individual journeys: significant events that caused a particular traveller to turn onto a different path, or to see the road he travelled with new eyes.

One such event concerns Jacob (Genesis 28). On the run, escaping from an angry brother who wants to kill him, Jacob lays down to rest one night only to find that the spot he's chosen is a portal to the heavenly world. He sees an open heaven, with angels commuting between heaven and earth. His reaction is typical: the next day he sets up a stone monument to commemorate his experience and gives it a name: *Bethel* – 'House of God'. My guess is that he was tempted to stay a few more nights in that place so as to repeat the experience, but I can imagine God appearing to him further down the road, calling to him in the distance: 'Come on Jacob! Let's get on with it! It's time to move on!'

I travelled once through Wales from northeast to southwest. At many road junctions I came across chapels: some simple boxes, some more grand, but all had a resigned air about them, like flotsam washed up on a beach after a storm. I'm sure they were built in good faith by enthusiastic Christians that had encountered God, but now the tide had turned – only the empty shells were left. Could it be that at one time God had moved powerfully in those places, but they'd failed to notice that He'd moved on?

Monument or movement?

God is calling us to a journey. If we stay still for too long the chances are we'll lose sight of Him. Our tendency though, is to set up a monument, however small – maybe to repeat a song this week because God seemed to like it last week – to work to a formula instead of entering a conversation. It's like Peter who, when he saw Moses and Elijah glowing like isotopes on the hill with Jesus, wanted to build a shelter for them (see Mark 9:5). He was only displaying the usual human tendency to encase God in a human shelter. But God says, 'No, time to move on.'

You may be aware that a very small change in our genetic make-up can have an extraordinary effect. One small switch in our DNA that has inadvertently been flipped can lead to disease or congenital disorders. So it is with churches. Notice that only two small letters distinguish the words *monument* and *movement*. The enemy constantly tries to insert the letters *nu* into our genes, removing the letters *ve*. The result is churches happily camping out at places that God once visited back in the mists of history, never questioning the status quo, never considering that perhaps it might be time to break camp and move on – oblivious (or choosing to ignore) the fact that God is no longer there.

Remember the honeymoon
Consider for a moment the Feast of Shelters that we read about in Leviticus 23. This was one of the three major annual festivals that the nation of Israel observed. They were to gather branches and build makeshift survival tents; they had to move out of their houses and live in them for seven days. Why did God tell them to do this?

> *'This will remind each new generation of Israelites that their ancestors had to live in shelters when I rescued them from the land of Egypt.'*   (Leviticus 23:43)

What God is saying here is this: 'Let's remember the honeymoon. Let's remember how we walked together hand in hand and I looked after you. Don't get too stuck in your ways. Remember, I really love you! I looked after you then – I'll do it again.' This theme surfaces regularly in the stories and songs of Israel, as if God wants to constantly remind them of His unfailing love and the need to maintain a vibrant and immediate relationship.

My own honeymoon with the Holy Spirit, as I may already have mentioned, began in Norway. I'd teamed up with an

Australian and we decided we would hitchhike overland to Australia. In order to see as much of the world as possible we started our journey in Norway, arriving one wet summer's day in Kristiansand on the south coast, where we immediately headed north towards the Arctic Circle. I could tell you many stories. It was a very hand-to-mouth existence, and very immediate in the sense that life would take a different direction depending on who picked us up that day. I learned to trust God for the basics. Being a hungry, male twenty-year-old, food was one of the highest priorities. I remember one day finding sausages in the gutter (still wrapped in plastic, you'll be relieved to know!). We took them home, cooked them, and lived to tell the tale. I saw this as God's provision for us. On another occasion I remember mentioning to my friend that we had not had a good meal for some days. The driver of the next car that picked us up (who happened to be the lead trumpeter from the Oslo Philharmonic) turned to us and said: 'Are you hungry?' Stupid question, really. Within minutes, we were dining well at a very nice restaurant. It was great!

Now that I have three kids, a leather couch and a Volvo, I worry that I'm getting too set in my ways. God often says to me, 'Remember the honeymoon, John.' It's my personal goal to live as much by faith as possible and to do mad things for God. It's much better than being bored!

Examining the foundations

So, now that we know change *is* here to stay, how can we manage change in our churches? One of the questions I'm asked repeatedly is this: 'We want to try out some new ideas in our services, but a lot of people get offended very easily. What can we do?'

Well, it may seem obvious, but before you build a building you have to dig the foundations. If you're building an extension or doing some major alterations, you need to check first of all that the foundations can take it. If not, you need to do some strengthening work. If you're adding an extension or a new attic room, you need to work out how this will tie in with the old building – new walls have to be structurally tied to the old. You need to know if the existing building is solid enough to take the extra weight.

Now all buildings – at least the ones that are standing – have foundations, but the thing about foundations is that you never see them. Apart from the fact they're under the building, very often they are covered by the debris of the centuries. I think you understand what I'm getting at. Like good archaeologists we need to carefully dig down to expose our history, carefully brushing away loose sand to expose the deep foundational stonework. We need to do what Nehemiah did when he decided to rebuild the Temple in Jerusalem after seventy years of neglect.

A structural survey

> 'I slipped out during the night, taking only a few others with me. I had not told anyone about the plans God had put in my heart for Jerusalem. We took no pack animals with us, except the donkey that I myself was riding. I went out through the Valley Gate, past the Jackal's Well, and over to the Dung Gate to inspect the broken walls and burned gates. Then I went to the Fountain Gate and to the King's Pool, but my donkey couldn't get through the rubble. So I went up the Kidron Valley instead, inspecting the wall before I turned back and entered again at the Valley Gate.'
>
> (Nehemiah 2:12–15)

Nehemiah's first priority was to carry out a detailed structural survey, but it's interesting to note that he did it under the cover of darkness, without telling people what he planned to do. So often I see creative people blasting into a church with bucketloads of ideas without having first done their homework. It reminds me of the time we were having some work done on our house and the plasterer turned up while we were still in bed!

Plans and visions often develop in darkness, when you're in bed reflecting on the things that happened that day. They develop in the quiet times, deep in our hearts where no one else sees except the Holy Spirit. Like a plant that does quite a lot of growing beneath the surface before it breaks out into the light of day, dreams and visions need a gestation period. Even Jesus, who surely could lay claim to having the most amazing plan of all time, is described as growing up *'before him like a tender shoot'* (Isaiah 53:2 NIV). He waited patiently for thirty years before going public. We see also that a key step in this process is fasting and prayer. Nehemiah's first reaction when he hears about the devastation of the Temple is to cry out to God, *'When I heard this, I sat down and wept. In fact, for days I mourned, fasted, and prayed to the God of heaven '*(Nehemiah 1:4).

So, although you might be bursting with creative vision, or seething with judgemental frustration, my advice is to take your time before you bless the church leaders with your wisdom. A baby born prematurely is much less likely to survive.

Don't work alone

Consider something else in this story. Although Nehemiah says that he hadn't told anyone else about his dreams, he says, *'I slipped out during the night, taking only a few others with me'* (Nehemiah 2:12). My advice is to test your dreams and visions on a few like-minded people before you go too far. Not only is it a biblical principle to work in teams, but also this will act as safety net to prevent you doing something you might later regret. I am so thankful for the people that God has put around me. I'm sure that without those people who were brave enough to challenge me about certain things, I would have done something really stupid by now. (We'll explore team working later in Chapter 9.)

Get planning permission

After much prayer and fasting, whom did Nehemiah go and see? Well, he went to his boss, the king, to get planning permission. Before you go *too* far down the road of rebuilding your church it might be wise to tell your pastor or priest! Exactly when you do this is up to you. It would certainly pay to do your research first, but whenever you do decide to 'go public' talk to the pastor first. He or she is the person who has to carry the can for the church so you need to start there. So often, creative people will stir up turbulence in a church and, instead of bringing about a change of course, it more often than not results in capsize. You need to work under the authority that God has placed over you.

So, let's return to the foundations. What I want to try and give you in the next few sections is an understanding of the foundations of worship (or any other area of ministry), and ways that you might be able to evaluate them. This is the first step in bringing about change. We need to consider four things that make up the building and then look at practical ways of putting plans into practice. Church builders are familiar with these principles, but I want to try and apply them specifically to worship.

Values

Values, like foundations, are unseen and yet they support the whole building. When we looked at the subject of idolatry we saw how values like 'an annual holiday' could become the basis for behaviour – the working of excessive overtime and so on – which led to the value being fulfilled. In the same way good values are (or should be) the foundation for our behaviour in worship.

Typical examples of values in worship are:

- Being culturally relevant.
- Historical tradition.
- The preaching of the Word.
- Intimacy.
- Spiritual life as opposed to 'the flesh'.
- Physical expression through the arts.
- Not going on too long.
- Not being restricted by time constraints.

Values are conceptual rather than practical, but they have a big influence on the ideas and principles we accept and, therefore, on the way we behave. Values can obviously conflict, but more often than not it's the practical outworking of values that causes problems. Take the first two, for example. At first sight they might seem mutually exclusive, but there may well be ways of making historical tradition relevant to today's generation.

Sometimes values do conflict and it's then that you need to sit down (with the group) and decide which one is correct or, as is more often the case, which is the priority. The last two are examples of this. Where you do get value conflicts it's often a matter of deciding which is the most important, or which is most biblical (not always possible – if it's not obvious you could ask whether it's *un*-biblical), or whether the two can happily co-exist. Worship values obviously don't exist in isolation either, so in a church situation where, say, we value both 'intimacy' and 'children' we would have to somehow work out a compromise. Much of the heat can be taken out of conflict by explaining the underlying reasons why a certain thing is done in that way.

Priorities

As we come a bit higher up in the building we get *priorities*. Priorities are the practical results of values, so they're not just concepts but particular things that we make a priority in our lives. So going back to the value of being culturally relevant in worship, one of our priorities might be that we try not to alienate 'normal' people that come to our services.

Practices

Now we're beginning to get more practical and more visible because *practices* are, as their name suggests, the practical results of values and priorities. They are symbols of what we believe. So, in our quest to be culturally relevant and not wishing to alienate people, our practice might be to avoid using archaic language. Tolerating (or even encouraging!) nicely distorted electric guitars might be another outcome.

Programmes

The final stage in our building project is to put *programmes* in place, which will give structure and momentum to our practices. Programmes, I suppose, are more like the frame of the building that helps hold the walls in place. The problems come when programmes and practices no longer link back to underlying values, or, when those underlying values themselves are no longer current. Let's look at an example.

I was once visiting a church in the north of England and my main reason for going was to check it out, as a friend of mine attended a similar church in another town. Being new, I walked rather hesitantly through the door, and found a room packed with people talking at the tops of their voices. I guess there were maybe three hundred people there. After a few minutes I found myself being questioned by a beautiful young girl who appeared very interested in me. A pleasant start, I thought. She then revealed that she was the 'Guest Liaison Officer' and wondered if she could take my name and introduce me later in the service? Somewhat reluctantly I told her my name and she disappeared into the crowd. I sat right at the back when the service got under way (as you do); loud worship (quite fun) was followed by lots of notices (quite boring). After the notices she approached the platform: 'We have three guests with us this morning,' she announced, 'and I'd like you to give them a warm welcome.'

Enthusiastic clapping ensued. 'The first is ...' To my horror she announced the name of the first guest who was then obliged to stand in his place, confirm his name, followed by a brief speech which included – in his case – greetings from his home church in another town. I was next, and I mumbled a few words, wondering why my friend couldn't have been an Anglican. I wasn't sure, to be honest, if I had been welcomed or vetted.

Here the underlying *value* was 'we value guests'. The *priority* flowing out of that was 'we want to make our guests feel welcome'. The *practice* was to publicly do this and the *programme* was to appoint a Guest Liaison Officer to co-ordinate the welcoming process. The main problem here (in my opinion) was the underlying value. Rather than 'we value guests', it was in fact 'we value guests from other churches in our own denomination'. If they really *did* value random guests then I don't think the programme was suitable. If we gave them the benefit of the doubt and accepted 'we value all guests' as a recognised value, then it is clear that the practices and programmes needed a complete re-think.

This is what I mean by brushing away the dust and revealing the real foundation. My fear is that much Christian practice cannot stand up to such scrutiny and that when we begin to expose the values we hold dear, we'll find that many have become twisted and distorted by time and are in fact not values that we can believe in at all. Many, as I have said, are rooted in soil that has become contaminated – poisoned by ungodly, unbiblical philosophies and selfish motives. Others sink deeply into historical sub-soil that has no relevance to modern life. It's time we began to build on conscious truths that we can believe in rather than unconscious assumptions that have lost their relevance. And at the risk of repeating myself, we must once again bring God's Word into the foundations of our churches.

Using the tools

Write down your values

I hope that this kind of analysis will enable you to get to the root of issues and help you to re-evaluate practices. It certainly underlines the need for well thought-out, articulated foundational values, particularly if you are setting up a new ministry project. When I was launching the Creative Worship Centre here in Manchester I spent a good deal of time identifying and listing our values which then formed the basis of a five-year business plan. Half of them were imported from the vision document that had been put together by the senior pastor (shared values are essential if you are part of a wider context), the other half particularly related to worship and the arts. Just so you understand the kind of things we're talking about, church values here at the Manchester Vineyard include:

- The pursuit of God – knowing and experiencing His presence.

- The Kingdom of God – demonstrated by the active work of the Holy Spirit.

- Relationships – we value relationship above programmes.

- Simplicity – we aim to be functional and straightforward.

And so on. On top of these generic church values, I added the following worship-related values:

- The local church – we don't want to start a para-church organisation.

- Mercy – the idea that 'mercy triumphs over judgement' is central to our style of leadership and worship.

- Excellence – we believe in excellence in all we do (not perfection).

- The arts – we value creative gifts that allow individual and communal expression.

Other values included anointing (and I defined what I meant by that term), personal holiness, and prophecy.

Develop a long-term strategy
Most people over-estimate what they can do in one year, but under-estimate what they can do in five. We don't have much time to go into details of how to plan and strategise here, but let me mention a few ideas.

Whether you're starting a new ministry or you've inherited someone else's project, spend a few moments to ask yourself: 'Where do I want to be in five years time?' When I say a few moments, a more realistic time frame would be one complete day away. In the first instance, it's good to work alone as well. Now is the time to dream your dreams, to think big. It is important not to limit your thinking by being too pragmatic – just go for it! It's good at this stage to recall any prophetic words that you've been given, or any particularly meaningful scriptures. In particular, try and identify any themes that have been with you consistently over the years – the kind of things that have stood the test of time.

Begin then to sift through your list of crazy ideas and ask yourself: 'What do I need to do to achieve this? What steps do I need to take? How do I get there from here?'

Be ruthless in your evaluation

If you've stepped into someone else's shoes – say you've been appointed worship coordinator and have inherited a motley selection of 'would-be's' and 'has-been's' that make up the worship team – don't be afraid to be ruthless in your evaluation of the current situation. The bottom line is that whatever you do you'll probably be unpopular. John Wimber once observed: 'Being a leader is like volunteering to be ugly.' You'll not be able to please everybody, so you might as well get used to it! Good, sensitive Christian souls (as you probably are) don't want to rock the boat. They want to be nice to people. It's at times like these you need to remind yourself that worship is not about being a man-pleaser and the primary reason why churches exist is to influence those who aren't in it yet. Church is not a 'bless-me club'.

So, as you ponder on how things are, ask some basic questions. The first is, 'What business are we in?' The second is, 'How's business?' In management we sometimes talk about 'dials and levers', and it's good to identify those too. Dials are indicators; they help you take the temperature, to find out how much pressure there is in the system. Levers are things that you pull to adjust the process and trim efficiency, or to change course – as in my analogy of the tiller on a boat.

As you ponder your situation, try and identify what values are underpinning your practices and programmes. Try and identify areas where programmes are no longer serving the church as they should – areas where *what you do* no longer represents *what you believe*.

So, what business *are* we in? The trite answer is to say 'leading worship', or 'leading people into God's presence'; I think we need to be more specific than this, to break 'business' down into smaller areas. You might list things like: 'helping people to worship on Sunday mornings'; 'providing worship leaders for home groups'; 'training and releasing new worship leaders'; 'broadening the worship horizon in the church'; 'helping people understand more about what worship really is', and so on.

Then ask the second question: 'How's business?' Here an understanding of the 'dials' is useful. If your goal is to lead the congregation into God's presence on a Sunday morning, how might you evaluate your success? What feedback are you getting from the congregation and the leaders? How might you gauge the spiritual temperature? If your church aims to welcome outsiders, how accessible is worship for them? Then try and identify the levers that you might need to pull. In this last example, the whole area of presentation should be considered: just as a guest would not feel comfortable in your house if it was a complete mess, so he would not relax in your church if the projected words were illegible, the stage was a rat's-nest of tangled wires, and so on. We'll consider such practical things in a later section, but for now let's consider the next step.

Going public

Once Nehemiah had done his survey, spoken to the king and decided on his action plan, he went back to the king to get permission to do the work. He couldn't keep things secret any more: he had to go public. This is the scary stage – when you put your thoughts and plans down on paper and let other people see them. I feel like apologising for saying this (because it's so obvious), but unless you do this no one's really going to know what you're thinking. You can plan and scheme as much as you like, but unless you clearly communicate your vision you're wasting your time. Not only is it good to write things down, but also you need to talk about your vision – weave it into the fabric of your church. The first step in this process is to talk to your leader. Clarify your thinking as much as possible before you do this, having identified the root issues as we've discussed.

Now that the cat's out of the bag the fun begins. I heard someone once describe project development like this: 'Conception is really fun, gestation lasts a long time and is tedious, birth

is painful, and growth requires a lot of feeding and patience.'
Well, we're at the birth stage, so let's look at the how to manage
the pain.

Dealing with conflict

The story of Nehemiah is really inspiring because it is so
practical. In the early chapters of the book, we see Nehemiah
using his motivational gifts, mobilising teams of people to work
on different areas of the city walls. Although I've said some
negative things about man-made walls, you can't work without
setting some boundaries in place and the role of a leader is to
provide a framework within which people can work and develop
their gifts. Clearly, Nehemiah was a gifted leader because people
wanted to follow him. Let's consider three things that we can
learn from Nehemiah's approach.

Common sense, prayer and worship
Nehemiah faced opposition almost from the word go. What I
like about him is his practical spirituality. His first response is
usually to pray. Sometimes it's an off-the-cuff cry for help: ' . . . *so,
with a prayer to the God of heaven, I replied . . . '* (Nehemiah 2:4).
Sometimes it's time set aside: *'In fact, for days I mourned, fasted,
and prayed to the God of Heaven'* (Nehemiah 1:4). So when
opposition does come he's pretty confident that God is going
to see him through: *'The God of heaven will help us succeed. We his
servants will start rebuilding this wall'* (Nehemiah 2:20). There's a
stubbornness that I like about him – an inability to accept defeat
and the ability to see beyond the immediate chaos.

Combined with prayerfulness and vision, Nehemiah is not
afraid to use his common sense. When faced with opposition
he is politically astute and very practical, as in the time when he
sorts out the banking and commercial aspects of the project (see
Nehemiah chapter 5). There's nothing 'unspiritual' about using
common sense, but sometimes I wonder if Christians have
any brains at all! I've seen some extraordinary things in my
time. Like the time I was leading worship in a large meeting and
two stagehands carefully positioned a white projector screen
between the congregation and myself. I still had two more songs
to go and had to fly blind for the next ten minutes of worship.
When I asked them about this afterwards, I was told: 'We didn't

want to interrupt the flow of the meeting.' Fair enough, I thought, but a little more common sense wouldn't have gone amiss.

There's one incident I really like in Nehemiah chapter 8, and it's when they re-discover the Feast of Shelters. Ezra the scribe has been doing some research – examining the fine print of the law – when he makes a discovery. 'Goodness me, it's October!' he exclaims, 'time for the Feast of Shelters. Let's do it!' So they send all the people out to the surrounding countryside to gather branches and they have a seven-day party, camped on the roofs of their houses. Now what you need to remember here is that they're in the middle of a war zone with enemies not far away and a city that is only partly re-built. It's chaos out there, and yet they take the time to worship.

In your re-building programme God will probably remind you at various points along the way just to chill out and worship. It may seem irrational and contradict what I've just said, but we must allow God to override our common sense at times. Make worship a priority. Even if you personally feel war-damaged, or your church seems little more than a burned-out shell, *choose to worship*. If you wait until the work is finished you'll never do it and besides, God loves a sacrifice of praise.

When we devote time to prayer we begin to understand God's vision and timescale; when we make worship a priority we avoid a human focus; and when we use our common sense we recognise the need for God-inspired wisdom. With this foundation we can look conflict in the eye without feeling threatened.

Dealing with dry rot
Dry rot is my analogy for an endemic disease that eats at the structural integrity of a church. It requires drastic treatment and, more often than not, the removal of infected materials. It is therefore not a job for the unqualified. For example, a lot of Christians attend church not for what they can give, but for what they can get out of it. Many approach worship, stifling a yawn, with the attitude: 'I might worship a bit if the music's better than last week.' Sadly, the observation that worship is 'happy-clappy' with little real substance, or merely the observance of a ritual, is often well founded. For many people claiming to be Christians, the definition of worship is 'a weekly religious

ritual enacted for my benefit'. I've also come across some churches that organise their programmes to suit a small number of often older people who have held the reigns of power for too long. Other churches have degenerated into mere social clubs. These are symptoms of underlying disease. Dealing with such issues is beyond the scope of this book. They concern church government and leadership, and can only be addressed by the church leaders and, as we've seen, many such issues involve cultural change, which takes significant time and investment before results are seen.

Hopefully the analytical tools we've looked at will help you understand root issues, but when it comes to major surgery in any church this can only be accomplished by skilled pastoral leadership. My advice to people who find that they cannot work within the existing structures, and who see no likelihood of them ever being changed, is to leave. This is a decision that you need to take after a period of time, and with much prayer, but if at the end of the day you feel constantly frustrated and unable to serve the church wholeheartedly then you should consider moving on. This will probably be good for the church as well, because there's nothing worse for a leader than to have people who are constantly critical. Too often I meet Christians trapped in compromise who remain faithful only through a sense of duty. By all means stay and work for reform if that is what you feel God is calling you too, but you should at least consider the option of leaving.

Dealing with value conflicts

Groups of people are never homogenous so, like a marriage, there's got to be a certain amount of give and take. One person's 'nice song' is inevitably another's 'awful noise'. In cases of conflict, the first step is to try and understand what the underlying values are. Dig back down to the foundation and get to the root of the issues. Sometimes this alone – bringing values and priorities out into the light of day – will make clear a solution. I know of a church, for example, where the worship is led by a very raw and inexperienced youth band. Guitars are often out of tune and the polite way to describe it would be to say that the worship is characterised more by passion than finesse. This particular church places a high value on young people – they want to embrace them, encourage them, and train them up. So every

Sunday they let them loose on the congregation. They also value musical skill, but this (for them) is less of a priority. They value passion more than a veneer of respectability and as a result the youth work in that church has exploded over the last couple of years.

Typical conflicts that arise in worship look like this:

- We value simplicity so that people can easily worship. In practice, this means that we sing simple songs and encourage people to join in. However, we also value the arts, the creative diversity and complexity that reflect God's nature. In practice this means that we experiment with varied and unusual art forms.

- We value excellence on the basis that scripturally our sacrifices should be 'without blemish', so we aim for a professional standard of musicianship. However, we also value lay-involvement and the fact that we all have something to offer in worship, and so want to involve as many people as possible on the worship team.

I'll leave you to think about these as we continue.

The second step is to test values and practices against Scripture. This won't necessarily work in every case, but it may help to shed some light. There is what might be called scriptural 'non-negotiables' in worship: worship must honour God; it must be doctrinally and biblically sound; and (if the aim is to facilitate corporate involvement) it must encourage people to get involved, at least at some level.

The third step is to prioritise. Sometimes values, in themselves good, conflict. Take, for example, 'the priority of corporate worship' and 'the preached word of God'. In cases like this, just getting the issues out into the open will help resolve potential conflict. Explaining to the worship leader *why* he has to finish worship promptly at eleven o'clock makes the bitter pill easier to swallow.

Don't forget to do what Nehemiah did: soak the situation in prayer and defer to your leaders. There are many situations where there is no right or wrong; in such cases someone – the leader – has to decide and people need to have the maturity and humility to let the leader lead. Also, don't forget that clear communication in itself can defuse potentially difficult situations; don't just assume that people understand the whys and wherefores of what's going on.

Note
1. Michael Mayne, *This Sunrise of Wonder: Letters for the Journey* (Fount Paperbacks, 1995) p. 70.

Chapter 5

The Character of Worship

What does radical, Spirit-filled worship look like?

In Chapter 2 we saw that worship involves both bowing down and service, and we came up with a definition of worship: *worship is the expression of a love-relationship with Jesus.* We also said that we were going to look at three key questions: What is worship? What does it look like? And how do we lead people into it? Well, it's time we considered this second question: What does worship look like? What characterises real, Spirit-filled worship?

Three key things which have affected worship

When we looked at the three major streams of Western Christianity we saw how each one emphasised particular things based on their theological emphases, but that also there are some historical events that had a big impact on worship. I'd like to focus for a moment of just three of these, which have left their mark on the way we worship today.

The printing press

As Webber points out in his book,[1] the printing press helped to change the face of worship. Up until the sixteenth century worship was primarily symbolic. The sacraments – Mass and baptism being the most important – were supplemented by numerous visual aids: icons, statues, crucifixes, pageants, priestly vestments, prophetic acts and liturgical drama. Alongside these, stories and poems were used to convey truth. Some stories were simply a re-telling of biblical stories; others grew up as part of myth and tradition, like George and the Dragon or Robin Hood.

Round about the time when Luther was nailing his *Ninety-Five Theses* to the door of the Wittenburg church (1517), the first printing presses were beginning to mass-produce words for the first time. (In fact Luther's theses were printed and circulated without his knowledge.) Luther's studies of the Bible led him to rediscover some basic truths that we often take for granted – the centrality of the Bible, justification by faith, the role of grace and the priesthood of believers – and this changed the face of Christianity, launching the Reformation. In particular, it was a reaction against abuses in the Church of his day. The spotlight once more began to shine on the Bible and soon it was being published and distributed on a scale hitherto unknown. In England, the path that had started with Wycliffe's audacious translation in the 1380s (he was burnt posthumously at the stake for his trouble!) reached a turning point when King James authorised an official version in 1606.

This represented a quantum shift in the nature of worship. Instead of stories and symbols, *words* played a much more important role. Some would argue, as I've already mentioned, that the Bible simply replaced images and icons as the idol in worship. The heritage of this period is both positive and negative; yes, the unchanging truth of God's Word was restored to its rightful place, but the downside was a reaction against all things symbolic or mystical. We are still living in the fallout of Calvin's assertion that our imagination is 'corrupted fantasy'.

Rationalism

The mid-nineteenth century saw the rise of rationalism. Now, the Bible itself was under attack from both liberal theologians and secular scientists, and the response from the Church was, more often than not, to hide behind dogma rather that to engage in debate. A statement from a Congregationalist minister in 1834 is typical when he stated that: 'the Bible and the Bible alone is the religion of dissenters'.[2] He goes on the contrast the 'Rock of Holy Scripture' with the 'quicksand of human opinion'. This period was arguably the beginning of divorce proceedings between belief and reality. You get the impression that worship became escapist in nature. Songs about the 'sweet by and by' tried to ignore the realities of creeping secularism:

'O how sweet to look beyond with a yearning deep and
     fond
To that city with bright mansions on high;
What a happy happy throng, there will raise the victor's
     song
When the Saviour call us home by and by.'[3]

But rationalism was also affecting worship in other ways. There
was a general consensus that anything that could not be understood could not be from God, since God had given us the gift of
intellect. Also, the rationalistic approach meant that worship
became very didactic, with songs that reminded people of their
duties, or the error of their ways. Moody and Sankey's 'Renounce
the Cup' is a real tear-jerking example of this, telling how a
drunkard's behaviour leads to the tragic break-up of his family.
The idea that you could draw close to God in intimacy would
have been foreign to a lot of people at that time.

As this is fairly recent history we find strands of these practices
woven through much of our current worship. In particular, we
are left with a legacy of hymns that speak a lot *about* God, but
seldom express love directly to him.

Post-modernism

Another major shift in thinking was the advent of post-
modernism. Post-modernism is a rather loose term, which describes a reaction – you've guessed it – against modernism. The
'modern' period really started back in the 1600s when Descartes
began to demolish medieval and Renaissance thinking with his
focus on the rational mind. This was the beginning of the movement known as the Enlightenment that swept through much of
Europe, culminating in the rationalistic pride of the nineteenth
and early twentieth centuries. Post-modernism rejects absolute
truth and questions certainty. A typical example of this is in
linguistics where words are robbed of their obvious meaning,
opening the way for bizarre interpretations of previously self-
evident texts. Truth became subjective: 'What's important is what
is true *for me*.'

What's this got to do with worship? Well, many Christians are
rightly worried by the cavalier attitude to truth: if you take away
absolutes you end up with a pluralistic church that happily
embraces all sorts of weird and wonderful doctrines and practices.

(An example of this is Rowan Williams, the new Archbishop of the Church of England, being happy to wear the robes of an honorary Druid priest in Wales.) But the main problem is that the focus on *me* means that worship can become very self-centred. We evaluate our services by asking ourselves: 'Was it good for *me*?' Did *I* enjoy it?

Post-modernism does, however, offer many opportunities: people are willing to be open to ideas that they would previously have dismissed as 'obviously unscientific', and it has also opened the door to a renewed emphasis on spirituality. Now that the god of rationalism has been demoted, there's a real opportunity for worship to become passionate again. To put it another way: worship is becoming less of an intellectual exercise and more of a love affair.

Rebuilding David's tent: getting back to God's model

> *'In that day I will restore the fallen kingdom* [or tent] *of David. It is now like a house in ruins, but I will rebuild its walls and restore its former glory.'*   (Amos 9:11)

I don't know how you felt after reading the last three historical sections, but I feel really excited to be living now at the beginning of this new millennium. We have a unique opportunity to take the best things from historical tradition, as well as the best things from the different streams of Christianity, and weave then into a beautiful fabric of praise and worship. It may possibly become our wedding gown. If the Church really is the bride of Christ, then surely these last days will reveal a beauty that we've not yet experienced. What I want to do now is to suggest some threads that may be woven into this fabric as new meets old, and God prepares His bride for eternity.

David's tent
What was so special about the 'fabric' of David's tent? What is it anyway? Why does God want to restore it? Before we answer these questions, I guess we need to look at why it says 'tent' (or the more old-fashioned word 'tabernacle') in some translations, and 'kingdom' in others.

'David's tent' is really a euphemism for 'David's line' – David's dynasty, if you like. This is why it is translated 'kingdom' in more recent versions. You remember that God had made a promise to David that he would never lack an heir to the throne – that his kingdom would, effectively, be eternal (see 1 Kings 2:4), and yet by New Testament times David's line was pretty much broken. Herod was claiming to be king of the Jews, but many despised him because he was half Arab and, what's more, he was more or less a puppet of the Roman occupiers. David's 'tent' had effectively fallen. However, Matthew then takes great pains to record genealogies which show that Jesus is legally the heir to David's throne – He comes from the line of David, and with His coming the tent is erected again. God hasn't forgotten His promise.

But does this verse (which is quoted by James in Acts 15) only mean the political restoration of David's dynasty? I don't think so. You see, 'David's tent' is a phrase that reminds us of the tent that he built to house, albeit temporarily, the Ark of the Covenant. This meaning is valid as well because it would be impossible to restore the true kingdom of David without also restoring the worship that was central to it. Amazing worship was integral to the kingdom package – it was the hallmark of David's reign. So God's desire to rebuild the tent speaks of both these things.

Now it would be naive to think that God is simply going to bring back an ark and that we will all crowd round it in worship, and yet many aspects of David's worship speak volumes to us today. This is hardly surprising when you think that God promised David an eternal kingdom – if God had an eternal destiny for David's dynasty then He would have made sure that He had woven eternal attributes into the genetic code. Moreover, when Jesus came and 'sat on the throne of David' this was probably a more literal fulfilment of the prophecies than David had ever dared to imagine. The angel Gabriel made this clear when he appeared to Mary.

> *'He* [Jesus] *will be very great and will be called the Son of the Most High. And the Lord God will give him the throne of his ancestor David.'* (Luke 1:32)

So we need to look at what characterised David's worship. It gets pretty exciting!

On earth as it is in heaven

I don't know whether you've ever thought about this, but worship – along with love and the Word of God – will last forever (see 1 Peter 2:25; Isaiah 40:6–8 and 1 Corinthians 13:8).

It's one of those things that will never fade away but will spill over into eternity. If this is true, shouldn't we expect worship on earth to converge with the heavenly as we approach the end of time? What I mean is this: the Bible makes it clear that this life is a kind of training course for the life to come – that your faithfulness and the wise use of your talents will be rewarded and, based on your performance here on earth, you will be allocated certain responsibilities in the new heaven and earth. There's no point in investing in expensive training courses for people if you end up allocating them a completely different job – something totally unrelated to the course – so shouldn't we expect at least some of the skills we're developing here on earth to be transferable to heaven?

On this basis, worship must become more heavenly as we approach the final curtain. I find it hard to believe that the many boring services that I've had to endure over the years have equipped me for anything, other than perhaps to develop the gifts of patience and longsuffering. There has to be more to worship than this, particularly as Jesus encouraged us to pray that the Kingdom of Heaven would break into the here and now:

> 'May your Kingdom come soon.
> May your will be done here on earth,
>   just as it is in heaven.'   (Matthew 6:10)

It seems that David – a man 'after God's own heart' – somehow understood this and decided to pattern his worship after the heavenly model, doing things which were radical and audacious, at times setting aside completely time-honoured traditions that had shaped worship practices in previous centuries. We need to learn some lessons from David's stubborn refusal to be a conformist.

The significance of the Ark – the presence of God

In what ways did David's worship reflect heavenly worship? Before we look into this we need to zoom out a bit and look at the wider picture. The Ark was where heaven touched earth for the Israelites – the place where God's glory lived. In this respect it was a metaphor for Jesus, pointing to the One who would come that would be God's visible presence on earth (see Colossians 1:17–19). Moses had made it according to very specific God-given plans some four hundred years before David's reign; plans which were a copy of a heavenly reality, for in Revelation we read:

> *'Then, in heaven, the Temple of God was opened and the Ark of his covenant could be seen inside the Temple.'*
>
> (Revelation 11:19)

The Ark was carried by the Israelites as they made the tortuous journey from Egypt towards the Promised Land, and housed in a portable tent where it was placed in the *'Most Holy Place'* (Exodus 26:34), an area hidden by a veil that only Moses was allowed to enter. Even Aaron – Moses' priestly brother – was warned to keep his distance *'or he will die'* (Leviticus 16:2 NASB). And the reason? *'For I will appear in the cloud over the mercy seat'* (Leviticus 16:2 NASB).

God intended to be there in person, and the penalty for entering God's presence was certain death. This was widely understood in the culture and must have sent a shudder of fear through those who had to work in the vicinity. To cut a long story short (see Connor's book if you want to study this further),[4] the Ark eventually ended up at the house of a guy called Obed-edom (see 2 Samuel 6:1–11), but not before numerous people had died, either from looking into the Ark or treating it in the wrong way. It was a scary thing to have around! This makes it all the more astonishing to find the Ark taking centre-stage in David's time, with priests ministering around it, with no veil to hide them from the consuming flame of God's presence (see 1 Chronicles 16:37).

God moves on again

But note this: even though David had requisitioned the Ark, worship carried on as normal around Moses' Tabernacle that had eventually ended up at a place called Gibeon (so for some time there were two tabernacles). Priests still offered sacrifices and went through the daily rituals at Gibeon, and yet they knew that God wasn't there any more. It must have been somewhat depressing. The path of Church history is full of branches where God's presence seems to part company with established religion. We should not be surprised as God's presence grows at the beginning of this new millennium to find that old religious models become increasingly irrelevant, if not obsolete.

If it is true, as I've suggested, that as we approach the end of time there will be a blurring of the boundaries between the temporal and the eternal just as there was in David's day, then we have much to learn from the way David approached worship. What might characterise worship as we enter a new millennium?

Supernatural awareness

It is unclear whether the Ark burned continuously with the flame of God's presence, or whether God only showed His glory occasionally. Either way, the Ark was the focus of worship, prompting David to write, *'I love your sanctuary, LORD, the place where your glory shines'* (Psalm 26:8). What's more, everyone could see God's glory now that the veil had been removed: it was no longer the initiated few that were allowed to enter God's presence. New millennium worship will be characterised by an awareness of the supernatural. First of all there will be a longing for the genuine article, for a real encounter with God and secondly, an increased spiritual awareness will result in more sight and insight into what's really going on around us. The challenge for us will be to embrace the supernatural without being seduced into subjectivism; to remain wedded to biblical truth and to keep our eyes focused on Jesus.

For the last four years, we in the Manchester Vineyard have led a worship retreat in the Czech mountains. During the first event in 1999 we were worshipping when something extraordinary happened. It was during an evening celebration when some sixty musicians had gathered for prayer and worship. We were meeting in a ski lodge in a beautiful wooded valley. From the windows we could see the ski slopes that cut paths through the pine trees, curving down to level out at the foot of the valley near our hotel. It was dark by the time we started worship, and for some time we had been crying out in intercession for the Czech nation. We then started singing. After a short time someone in the front row began to clap, keeping time with the music, and as I looked at him I knew that somehow God was in this. Don't ask me how I knew. I signalled to the band to stop playing, but told the drummer to keep going. Soon, the whole room-full of musicians was clapping in unison, four beats to the bar. No one broke rank: the rhythm was a powerful beat of unity. I knew something was going on that I could not see because I could sense a change in the air – an intensity in the worship. A friend of mine was clapping with his eyes closed, standing next to the widow. As we locked into the rhythm he was puzzled by a sound coming from beyond the hotel, from the mountain opposite. It sounded like marching feet keeping time with our clapping. He turned to look out of the window and was shocked to see a company of angels, numbering in the thousands, marching down the ski slope, the light of their presence shining into the pine trees on either side. I did not see this, but at that moment I felt an extraordinary thrill run through me, and some verses from Isaiah came to mind, so I read them out. The passage finishes with these words:

> '*And as the* LORD *strikes them* [his enemies]*, his people will keep time with the music of tambourines and harps.*'   (Isaiah 30:32)

For a moment God had allowed us, like Elisha's servant (see 2 Kings 6:17), to see what was really going on around us. We will return to this passage in Chapter 10 because I believe it is one of the most significant and relevant passages regarding the kind of worship we can expect to see as the end of this age approaches. Since that time we have had numerous encounters with angels, and I know that one particular angel is always at my side when I lead worship. Such things should not surprise us. Not only is the Bible full of angels, but it also seems that God particularly mobilises them when significant historical events are about to happen.

Sight and insight
The operation of prophetic gifts depends on what could be called sight and insight. God will open our eyes (and ears), and we'll become much more aware of the supernatural realm. This is the gift of sight. Insight is the gift of prophetic wisdom to know what to do with what we're seeing. This story is just one example of the ways that God reveals things to us. For too long the Church has been flying blind, but now I believe God wants to give us back this gift of prophetic sight. We should not be surprised at a

marked increase in the exercise of spiritual gifts in these days and increasing dramatic signs of God's presence in the Church. As word gets around that God is in the house, people will be queuing up to get in.

The focus of worship must be Jesus

A brief warning before we move on: as with any gift, there is a danger that we fall in love with the gift and forget the giver. Church history is full of movements that went off the rails because they became over-enamoured with the glitz and glamour (or power) of revelation, instead of focusing on Jesus who alone is worthy of our worship and who shines with *'the glory of the only Son of the Father'* (John 1:14). This should be a warning to us. Just as the Ark was central to David's worship, so Jesus should be central to ours.

Intimacy

The second attribute of new millennium worship is intimacy. The lack of veil in David's tabernacle was amazing and very significant. As we have seen, it was such a daring approach to worship that it must have been God-inspired. I don't think David would have dared to go the route he did unless he'd felt that he had heard very clearly from God, particularly since he was indirectly responsible for the death of Uzzah when they had tried to transport the Ark on a cart instead of carrying it in the prescribed manner (see 2 Samuel 6). At that time David was full of good intentions but he also forgot to ask God what He wanted.

Carrying the presence of God

Let's just take a quick diversion and look at this incident. David had decided to bring the Ark back to Jerusalem, so he built a new cart to carry it. The procession set off towards the city with two men called Uzzah and Ahio keeping a watchful eye on it. The Bible recounts how at one point the oxen drawing the cart stumbled; the Ark was in danger of falling so Uzzah *'put out his hand to steady the Ark of God. Then the Lord's anger blazed out against Uzzah for doing this, and God struck him dead beside the Ark of God'* (2 Samuel 6:6–7). Intimacy is perhaps less attractive than it was a few moments ago.

The Ark was never designed to be carried on a cart; it was supposed to be carried on the shoulders of the priests by means of long poles that were threaded through rings on either side. Yes, the Philistines, the enemies of Israel, had sent the Ark back to Israel on a cart, but they didn't know any better. This is like people today who desperately try to 'move God' by getting involved in false religions and strange New Age myths. There's only one way that we can get close to God, then as now, and that's by following His instructions. Even churches are guilty of building 'new carts' at times: doing things which are entirely modelled on secular practice in the vague hope that by being culturally aware God will be impressed. They forget that there are some things that God has made very clear.

The names of the two helpers here are significant. Uzzah means 'strength' and Ahio means 'brotherly'. It can be so easy to put together worship programmes that rely on human strength or simply good ideas put forward by 'brotherly' committees and forget the divine dimension. My point is this; we must be careful that intimacy with God is not simply over-familiar irreverence, what C.S. Lewis described as treating God as 'the bell-hop of the universe'. The opposite should be true: that the closer we get to God the more we are in awe of His divine majesty and power. David got this message because the next time the Ark was moved he bent over backwards to do everything right. He gingerly made his way towards Jerusalem taking only six steps at a time, stopping every seventh step to make a sacrifice.

With this in mind, do you still want to be intimate with God? Well, as the sayings goes, it would be rude not to. You see, Jesus literally went through hell for us in order to give us direct access to God – to make intimacy with God possible. He paid the ultimate price to take the veil away. Paul summarises it like this:

'But whenever anyone turns to the Lord, then the veil is taken away. Now, the Lord is the Spirit, and wherever the Spirit of the Lord is, he gives freedom. And all of us have had that veil removed so that we can be mirrors that brightly reflect the glory of the Lord. And as the Spirit of the Lord works within us, we become more and more like him and reflect his glory even more.'

(2 Corinthians 3:16–18)

We cannot reflect the glory of God unless we, like Moses, get close enough to the firelight. We need to watch out that we don't draw the religious curtains and block out God's flame. Intimacy with God is not so much a sentimental feeling as a choice to live in God's presence and stay close to Him.

As we read John's gospel it is striking how John is always in on the action; he chooses to stay close to Jesus and is there at most of the significant events in the life of Jesus. Significantly, he is the only one of the twelve male disciples recorded as attending the crucifixion. We would not normally consider this to be an intimate moment, and yet that is exactly what it was. We should not equate intimacy with sentimentality or an absence of pain; sometimes the choice to be intimate will lead us into difficult situations, yet by the very nature of our choice we can be sure that Jesus will be there. The result of John's choice to stick close to Jesus was that he was known as *'the disciple whom Jesus loved'* (John 13:23). I would love this to be my epitaph.

Worshippers in the new millennium will find their day-to-day lives increasingly impacted by God as they make this choice. Corporate worship will become a living encounter with the burning presence of God, and we will see an increase in locations worldwide where Christians will gather in non-stop adoration around the throne of God.

Worship is a planned priority
In the eighties, here in England, there was a bit of a backlash against planned services, mainly because we were so bored with dull religious routines. Spirituality became equated with spontaneity, and services were often pretty chaotic as a result. As a worship leader in those days I often didn't bother to prepare for services; I'd just 'go with the flow', picking songs at random and fielding prophecies like a batsman facing an automated bowling machine. I was never sure which direction the next ball was coming from. This was a great training ground and I soon learned how to adapt quickly to changing circumstances. But it had a big downside. I think it was Gerald Coates who described this as a 'subjective binge', warning that we were in danger of losing sight of reality. He was right. We lost touch with scriptural foundations and began to drift around on a sea of subjectivism. There was lots of effervescence in our services, lots of surface activity, but little depth or substance.

Contrast this with worship in David's time. When reading Chronicles you are left with a vivid impression of order; nothing, apparently, was left to chance. It seems that David had put the considerable skills he had learned as a king and military strategist to good use. We read of the rotas that he put together for priestly service (twenty-four shifts); the division of the musicians into three companies under the supervision of gifted leaders; the appointment of gatekeepers (stewards) to oversee the practical management, and so on. As we step back for more of an overview we see how worship was the epicentre of an administration that had international influence. It was anything but random in nature.

The Ark was central to everything; it was the locus of worship – a pivotal point drawing all activities back to itself. Surrounding the Ark was a ring of ministering priests and musicians whose brief was '*to give thanks to the* LORD, "*for his faithful love endures for ever*"' (1 Chronicles 16:41). Surrounding them were the gatekeepers, each assigned a particular location to look after and beyond them, political and military leaders. The people of Israel found their identity in worship, and as a result the nation of Israel took centre-stage in international affairs, attracting tribute and admiration from distant nations. So what began as a simple focus on a small box – albeit a box containing the presence of God – resulted in an international ministry that affected the known world.

Churches that not only survive but also thrive in the new millennium will be those that have made worship a central priority and whose practices and programmes look to worship for meaning. They will not be fearful of discarding old models in favour of the new. However, new models will be well planned and executed with an increased understanding of the meaning of true worship. Such worship, unafraid to embrace the supernatural and combined with godly administration, will have a far-reaching impact that will help shape the wider culture. Instead of struggling to be culturally relevant, the church will set the trend for others to follow.

Artistic diversity and creativity

David's worship was an explosive renaissance of artistic creativity combined with extraordinary technological advances. The Temple was a state-of-the-art masterpiece of innovative design and, although his son Solomon eventually built it, David made all the plans and provisions before his death. Experts had to be flown in from Tyre to make the bronze castings, one of which – a large tank holding water for ceremonial washing called the Sea (see 1 Kings 7) – was probably one of the largest ever made. Not only was it large (it could hold eleven thousand gallons of water), but it was also beautifully ornate. The list of artists and artisans involved in the project represents just about all the known crafts and art forms of the day – it included sculptors, weavers, dyers, metalworkers, stonemasons, artists and so on. What's more, David himself invented musical instruments and no less than four thousand were used in the temple orchestra (see 1 Chronicles 23:5).

Sensory overload

Worship in the temple must have been an extraordinarily sensual experience. Candles and lamps burned and were reflected in ornate, gilded architecture; wave upon wave of new music would have washed over the spellbound onlookers; the smell of incense and anointing oil would have mingled with the odours of sacrifice, reminding worshippers of the cost of intimacy and everywhere a riot of colour and rich design assaulted the senses. The Queen of Sheba, not unused to extravagance, was said to be 'breathless' when she visited Solomon, saying: *'I didn't believe it until I arrived here and saw it with my own eyes. Truly I had not heard the half of it!'* (1 Kings 10:7).

John, in the book of Revelation, also struggles with sensory overload. Reading chapters 3 and 4 you get the impression that John cannot find adequate words to express the richness and diversity of his experience as he gazes through a door in heaven into the throne-room of God. His eyes are dazzled by the brilliance of the sight: rainbows like emeralds; twenty-four thrones around a central throne (made of gems) upon which is a lamb *'that had been killed but was now standing'* (Revelation 5:6); weird creatures covered in eyes; a sea of crystal in front of the throne in which is reflected lightning flashes and seven burning flames. His ears are similarly overloaded: voices like trumpets; peals of thunder; chants of worship; angels shouting with loud voices followed by the singing of *'thousands and millions of angels'* (Revelation 5:11). And even this isn't the end. The account finishes with a song sung by *'every creature in heaven and on earth and under the earth and in the sea'* (Revelation 5:13). Every creature! I don't think David thought his song 'Let everything that has breath' would be taken quite so literally (see Psalm 150).

Prophetic art

The marriage of artistic excellence with prophetic worship is powerful. We recently did a celebration here in Manchester where we experimented with art and technology. We used, among other things, a laser projector, a plasma ball, abstract video projection, face paints and masks, a graffiti wall, drummers, percussionists and experimental theatre. We also used theatre lighting and flame lights. It felt like a cross between a medieval fair, a New Age festival and a worship service. I suppose we shouldn't have been surprised, but God's presence was strong, with some saying that they'd entered into worship for the first time. A recurring comment was: 'Why can't church always be like this?' This is more than a passing question and needs to be addressed. Why is it that most of us are using church models that developed in the 1850s when the steam engine was the pinnacle of technology? Why is it that in a culture that is defined by visual images we communicate primarily with words? The answer lies in our fear of seduction and change.

I'll make the point again: if we can keep our eyes firmly focused on Jesus (as the writer of Hebrews encourages us to do) then I believe God will allow us be involved in some incredible art (and here I mean all the arts, not just visual art). It's a bit like *'seek first His kingdom and His righteousness, and all these things will be added to you'* (Matthew 6:33). It is easy to be seduced and sidetracked by the arts, which is probably why the likes of Calvin were so nervous about them. Art is powerful and shapes culture. Art cannot help but be prophetic – whether it prophesies about heaven or hell depends on the artist. This is why art brought into submission to Christ is a powerful force, and why Satan has done his best to uproot it from the Church and put in into the hands of reprobates.

A new renaissance

Worship in the new millennium will involve the restoration of powerful, prophetic art. The Church will once again find the means to express its love affair with the Creator Artist with a force and clarity that will confound the sceptics and spill out onto our city streets. Services will no longer involve rows of people facing the front with bored expressions on their faces. Worship will often involve simultaneous cameos as congregations split into smaller expressive groups. A sense of child-like wonder will thrill us as multi-coloured displays – some possibly coming directly from heaven – lead us into the throne-room of God. New music and new sounds will make the old songs sound tame and we will regularly smell the fragrance of Christ in our services as we worship together. God will allow this because we will be so in love with Jesus that none of these things will ever steal our hearts away from Him. And people walking in off the streets will realise that this is the reality they've been searching for.

What does artistic creativity involve?

We need to look a little closer at creativity in worship. Creative people often get a bad press and are viewed suspiciously, not just by Christians but also by society at large. They are said to be 'bohemian', meaning at best that they live socially unconventional lives, but more often than not meaning that they are time-wasting parasites. They are sometimes (as I have been) advised in no uncertain terms to get a 'proper job'. I find it sad that so many Christian artists have given up because of such harsh narrow-mindedness, all the more so because Christians, being nice people, tend to listen to their elders and betters, whereas your average heathen is too stubborn to take a blind bit of notice. So much of the best art is now non-Christian. Whereas the Church used to be the primary patron of the arts, that job has now been handed over to the 'god of this world'. Aristotle's famous words: 'give me the music of a nation and I will control its people', have sadly been fulfilled.

Now we don't have time to look at this subject in any detail, but let's just note here that where pastors and leaders do take the time and effort to mentor and disciple creative people, wonderful things result. Mike Bickle explores this in his book, *Growing in the Prophetic*.[5] For now, I want to look at the creative process in more detail.

The Holy Spirit
The creative process begins with the Holy Spirit.

> *'In the beginning God created the heavens and the earth. The earth was empty, a formless mass cloaked in darkness. And the Spirit of God was hovering over its surface.'*   (Genesis 1:1–2)

Whilst it's true that all people share something of God's creative nature, it seems that something special happens when someone gives their life to God in true worship. Once you become a Christian, *incredible* creative resources are at your disposal because, as Peter puts it, *'you will share in his* [Jesus'] *divine nature'* (2 Peter 1:4). I used the word 'incredible' on purpose because I meet so many Christians who live in creative poverty because they find God's promises 'incredible' – unbelievable. And because they don't believe that Jesus really will come up with the goods they live a life with a creative short-circuit – a spanner across the battery terminals. There is a fine line between incredulity and unbelief. You might not be able to get your head round the fact that the same power that raised Jesus from the dead lives in you (see Romans 6:4 and Philippians 3:10), nevertheless, choose to walk in that reality. To put it another way: the same Holy Spirit that hovered over the *'formless mass cloaked in darkness'* that was the newborn earth is the same Spirit that is hovering over you, urging you to creative extravagance, calling out for beauty to grow in the rich soil of your life.

Peter prefaces his comments by saying that this Christ-life within us, this creative power, will enable us to *'escape the decadence all around* [us] *caused by evil desires'* (2 Peter 1:4). You – the creative person that is you – doesn't have to live as a bohemian wreck, soaking up the values and decadence of the world around you. Salvation means stepping out of creative barrenness or depressive self-obsession into dynamic, Sprit-filled, creative life.

Why not take a few moments now and ask the Holy Sprit to flood through your being once again? Give Him permission to call out to the 'deeps' in your heart as He did at creation. Ask Him to renew the creative heart in you – maybe to get your intellectual understanding of these truths from your head down into your heart. I'd particularly like you to do this if you feel somehow short-circuited in your creativity. Ask the Holy Spirit to begin the work of restoring your creative heart.

Wisdom

Wisdom is the second ingredient of creative fruitfulness.

> *'By wisdom the* Lord *founded the earth; by understanding he established the heavens. By his knowledge the deep fountains of*

the earth burst forth, and the clouds poured down rain. My child,
don't lose sight of good planning and insight.'

(Proverbs 3:19–21)

I must confess to being slightly irritated when I tell people that
I'm a musician and I get the response: 'So, you're one of those
disorganised artistic types.' I know exactly what they're thinking
– that I drift through life in some kind of art-fuelled haze, and
although, as a Christian, they don't expect me to be on drugs,
the inference is that I might as well be. Yes, I know musicians
and artists who are hopelessly unwise and disorganised, but I
know accountants who are just as bad! So, just for the record I'd
like to state categorically: artists can be wise and organised
people, and often are.

In fact I would go much further than this. I see artistic gifts as
being almost synonymous with prophetic gifting. We'll develop
this more in the last section, but consider for a moment what the
prophetic gift entails. Yes, there is a revelatory element. God will
assault your senses or your mind with a particular truth that He
wants to bring to your attention, but it takes a lot of wisdom and
insight to know how and when to use this. The most gifted
prophets I know are those who not only have this ability, but who
also have biblical knowledge and human wisdom that allows
them to contextualise the particular word from God. They know
when to speak and when to hold their tongues. Like the Sons of
Issachar, they understand *'the times'* (1 Chronicles 12:32) – in
other words they have a grasp of history and current affairs.[6]

So a successful artist is one who is wise in the way that she
creates her art, but also wise is the way that the art is used. This is
particularly true for the worship leader who has to constantly
make on-the-fly decisions as to the appropriateness of contributions in a service. So, instead of seeing wisdom as the stifling
killjoy of creativity – the antithesis of artistic freedom – we
should welcome wisdom as our creative dance-partner:

'I [wisdom] *was the architect at his side. I was his constant*
delight, rejoicing [or playing, dancing] *always in his presence.'*

(Proverbs 8:30)

It is impossible to be filled with the Holy Spirit and not have
access to wisdom because wisdom is not only a gift of the Holy

Spirit, it is part of His nature. The old hymn rightly describes God as the 'immortal, invisible, God only wise'. Whether we embrace wisdom and understanding is another matter. I know many people who have plans to change the world but cannot even tidy their own bedroom.

Imagination

As seen, the Puritan distrust of the imagination permeates much of Western Christian thought, but like art, the imagination is only as perverted as the person who owns it. Furthermore, it's not as if we are capable of turning our imaginations off as if they were taps. Language itself depends on our ability to conceptualise abstract thought: the previous sentence would have made no sense to you unless you had the ability to imagine a tap! Imagination is an essential part of the human thought process.

It seems that creative people have the ability to shift up a gear or two when it comes to using their imagination and the creative process is essentially making public what was once just an internal concept; revealing what was hidden. Imagination is therefore also integral to the prophetic gift. 'To prophesy' literally means 'to tell forth' in the sense of revealing the hidden things of God (see Chapter 10). The artist or musician puts down on paper, canvas, or sound waves what was once just a 'figment of the imagination'.

I was struck by a passing comment in Dickens' *Hard Times*. He said this: 'there is something in the imagination of man that no amount of steam engines will satisfy'. Steam engines for Dickens were the height of technology (the romance of hindsight had yet to come); they loomed with massive presence and power and yet they had no soul. We might substitute computers instead.

A visit to Siberia had a similar effect on me. The town I visited had been cut into the Siberian wilderness – a concrete warren housing a million people. The town planners had designed it for maximum efficiency with, for example, underground walkways to provide protection from the harsh winter weather. And yet it was a town without a soul, without a smile: just faceless concrete throwing back the unforgiving summer sun. In the centre of the town there was a strange monument: a high-rise building towering over its neighbours, yet unfinished and roofless with a crane poking out from its centre like a giraffe trapped in a pen. The project had been nearing completion when the builders had realised that they had no way of removing the crane from the centre of the building. And so it still stands – a monument to the lack of imagination.

There is something about prosaic certainty, however useful, that leaves us cold; we long, as human beings made in the image of God, for the warmth of poetic uncertainty and artistic beauty. Why? Because cold certainty speaks only of human power and control; of religious boundaries; of clipped wings. Yet we were designed to rise up on wings like eagles, riding on the thermals of God's love, spinning into infinity and laughing. Sharing in the creative process.

Imagination is not an optional extra

Think about this for a moment: nothing exists under God's heaven that was not first imagined – nothing at all. So, without imagination we are doomed to a life of sterile conformity to what already exists. Like the man with the talent who buried it and found all he had to offer his master was the original gift, we are in danger of having to stand before the throne of God with empty hands and only an apology to offer.

Now the problem is that using the imagination is fraught with danger. It's a risky business, for the Bible makes it very clear that the heart of man is desperately corrupt. But didn't God take a big risk when He made His universe – when He went public with His vision? Yes, there was a risk involved as we know only too well, but in His imagination He saw the end result. The same is true as Jesus approached the cross:

> *'He was willing to die a shameful death on the cross because of the joy he knew would be his afterward.'*   (Hebrews 12:2)

So He calls us to follow His example and join the creative adventure.

Current (and, to be fair, older) worship songs are riddled with clichés, both lyrical and musical. We have grown used to artistic poverty; worship tapes that are little more than Christian 'musak'; wallpaper music that neither encourages adoration nor stimulates devotion. It is hardly the language of passionate love. Part of this reflects our culture where words have lost their value, but it is more a symptom of our addiction to mediocrity and our fear of failure. The Bible is a rich source of creative writing and poetry. Consider this passage and maybe compare it with words of worship songs that you know:

> '*My soul is among lions;*
> *I must lie among those who breathe forth fire,*
> *Even the sons of men, whose teeth are spears and arrows*
> *And their tongue a sharp sword.'*   (Psalm 57:4 NASB)

The richness and power of this language is evident: be inspired – begin to fire up your imagination and be creative once again. Let me leave you with a quote from someone who in my imagination has become a dear friend.

> 'When I no more can stir my soul to move,
> And life is but the ashes of a fire;
> When I can but remember that my heart
> Once used to live and love, long and aspire –
> Oh, be thou then the first, the one thou art;
> Be thou the calling, before all answering love,
> And in me wake hope, fear, boundless desire.'[7]

Excellence
At the end of each day's work, when God made the world, He took a step back and admired the result. Like an artist, He cast a practiced eye over His handiwork, perhaps wondering if something needed some adjustment during the following session. But there was never any need for this, because God saw that it was good. Excellence is the hallmark of God's creation.

Excellence or perfection?
Now, there is a difference between excellence and perfection. We need to strive for excellence – it is a scriptural principle that we should offer unblemished sacrifices – but only God can achieve perfection.[8] Perfectionism is a curse on many creative people, particularly for those who have followed a high level of classical training, because mistakes are viewed as failures. This in turn breeds not only fear (of making a mistake or deviating from the written score), but also a feeling that nothing is really ever acceptable. This is a problem common to any form of idolatry because idols make no provision for forgiveness: they always demand more of you; unable to forgive you for your human weakness, never satisfied with your sacrifices. Perfectionism will

consume your creativity until you are burned up. In contrast, sacrifices of praise offered to God through the cross of Jesus are accepted, as there is provision for forgiveness and room for human weakness. (The sad fact that many Christians make no provision for each other's weakness will be dealt with later.)

Mediocrity is endemic in church life. There are many reasons for this: the desire not to offend people, to include as many people in ministry as possible and so on, but the main reasons seem to be laziness and discouragement. In respect of laziness, it's almost as if having bought the insurance policy which gets you into heaven, you can now sit back and take it easy. Certainly creative people in the world seem to be much more dedicated to their calling than the average Christian. As far as discouragement is concerned, many musicians and artists that I know have just given up through feelings of unworthiness or of not being accepted. Many suffer from a melancholy spirit, often leading to depression. I'll deal with some of these issues later, but for now my encouragement to you is to *'lead a life worthy of your calling, for you have been called by God'* (Ephesians 4:1).

I feel a sense of urgency as I write this because the Church will not have a powerful voice in our culture until the artists, musicians and other creative people begin to take their rightful place in the body of Christ. You see, bad art cannot communicate profound truth: it's not that people reject the underlying message, it's that they never get to it. All they see is surface ugliness and banality. However good art can easily communicate profound evil, as the current assault on our senses bears witness. In Chronicles we read that *'Kenaniah, the head Levite, was chosen as the choir leader because of his skill'* (1 Chronicles 15:22). This has to be one of the qualities of a worship leader, so take time to develop your God-given gifts and don't be afraid to use them.

Variety and extravagance

> *'From the time the world was created, people have seen the earth and sky and all that God made. They can clearly see his invisible qualities – his eternal power and divine nature. So they have no excuse whatsoever for not knowing God.'* (Romans 1:20)

Art, as we have seen, reveals what was once hidden in the imagination of the artist. So it is with creation: this wonderful work of art reveals the invisible qualities of the great Creator Artist – it tells us something of His divine nature. One of the most obvious things it reveals is God's love of extravagant diversity. Did you know, for example, that there are 20,000 species of spiders? Known species, that is – new ones are constantly being discovered. The last estimate I heard of the number of galaxies in the known universe was 150 billion! Imagine how many stars, planets and moons that represents. It's as if God has no concept of conserving resources – He enjoys creating weird and wonderful things just for the sake of it. I also came across an interesting fact recently, that if the wealth and assets of the world were divided equally among all people on the face of the planet, each person would be worth around seven million US dollars! God has put more than enough wealth in the world to go round.

The spirit of poverty

Yet many Christians live under a curse of poverty. This has nothing to do with their circumstances, clearly even less to do with God, but everything to do with a mind-set of frugality. Some call this a 'spirit of poverty'. With closed hands fearfully gripping tightly onto what little they claim to own, they are unable to bless others. We need to learn to be more like the poor widow that looked after Elijah when the land was gripped in a punishing drought. She'd convinced herself she was at death's door and was about to make the last meal for herself and her son before lying down to die. Elijah persuaded her to give away what little she had, and as a result the blessing of God began to flow (see 1 Kings 17).

A spirit of poverty emasculates Western Christianity. How do we defeat it? Pray for more money? No! We need to begin to open our hands and give away what little we have. We need to begin to believe in the biblical principle of sowing and reaping. A song that I wrote a few years ago put it like this:

> 'Don't you know that the time has come to give it away,
>   give it away?
> Don't you know that if you hold on it'll slip through your
>   fingers?
> Don't you know that the time has come to give it away,
>   give it away?

Don't you know that if you hold on
It'll be gone – like mist in the morning
It'll be gone – a season that's turning
It'll be gone – a fire that's burning
Burning in the rain.'

Artistic poverty

When hard times come, funding for the arts is one of the first things to suffer. Why waste money on useless art when there are mouths to feed? It reminds me of post-war Britain where a gifted violinist was reduced to digging and re-filling holes in Hyde Park to show that he was really willing to work. It's no different when it comes to artistic worship: people view it as an unnecessary luxury because it doesn't immediately save souls or feed the poor. I've lost count of the number of conferences I've played at where thousands of pounds have been invested in the venue, the bookstall, the accommodation and catering for visiting speakers, the sound system, and yet little or no money has been made available to bless the musicians. The question we need to ask is this: 'Is this a biblical perspective?' I think not. The spirit of artistic poverty will only be broken as we choose to be extravagant investors in creative worship.

> 'If you give, you will receive. Your gift will return to you in full measure, pressed down, shaken together to make room for more, and running over. Whatever measure you use in giving – large or small – it will be used to measure what is given back to you.'
>
> (Luke 6:38)

God's almost wasteful extravagance is matched by variety. I'm sure it wasn't really necessary to create so many species of spider, but God thought it would be fun! So why is it that Christian worship is often so narrow and so limited? If David was so extravagant with his worship, why is it that we are so poor? Now it's true that if you were to take the whole expression of Christian worship as represented by the many shades and flavours of Christian tradition you would end up with a pretty diverse portfolio of art. You would have plainsong and rock music, icons and line drawings, gold leaf and concrete – an incredible spectrum of creativity. As you read this you probably agree that, yes, these are all valid expressions of Christianity. The problem seems to be that as individuals and local congregations we can't cope with too much expression which falls outside of our narrow tastes. We pay lip service to the concept of expressive diversity, but when it comes down to it we prefer to play it safe. There are invisible creative boundaries that we don't like to cross. I believe the time has come for us to genuinely embrace and encourage more diversity at a local level – to not just talk about it, but to actually do it. It's time to colour outside the lines. Like David dancing with all his might before the Ark, let's abandon human constraints and give God a real sacrifice of extravagant praise.

God's Masterpiece

I grew up in a church that emphasised the need for good works. We memorised Ephesians 2:10, which talks about being God's workmanship, created for good works. I remember washing cars to raise money for charity, visiting a local old people's home, cleaning the church building and so on. I even remember walking twenty-seven miles one night to raise money for refugees. (I was completely out of it the next day!) My under-standing of good works was limited to doing good deeds and I thought that this was the main way you showed your commit-ment to Christ. It wasn't until I was shown the true meaning of Ephesians 2:10 that the light came on. The New Living Bible correctly translates the Greek thus:

> *'For we are God's masterpiece. He has created us anew in Christ Jesus, so that we can do the good things he planned for us long ago.'* (Ephesians 2:10)

The word for 'masterpiece' is the Greek word *poiema* from which we also get the English word 'poem'. Each one of us is a handcrafted work of art, beautifully made. This will be even more evident when the stain of sin is finally washed off the face of the earth. This verse is really saying that we are the pinnacle of God's creative works. We are God's *chef d'oeuvre* – His Sistine Chapel ceiling, His Mona Lisa, His Fifth Symphony. So what does Paul mean when he says we are to do 'good things'? Surely it means that we are called to reflect the divine nature and get involved ourselves in the creative process. We have a mandate to be artistic in all that we do: it's a commission to share in the continuing development of creation. If this is not the case then we are not being true to our nature.

Creative sons and daughters

Now you might be thinking, 'We're not all artists, are we?' Well, I think we are. Our whole lives should be so suffused with the fragrance of Christ that everything we do, however mundane, has something of the divine artist in it. Everything we do should smell, however faintly, of His perfume. This is why Paul says: *'whatever you do, you must do all for the glory of God'* (1 Corinthians 10:31).

There is a curious phrase in Romans 8 where Paul says that creation is eagerly waiting for the sons of God to be revealed (see Romans 8:19). The implication is that the 'sons of God' are somehow lying dormant, as if we – assuming we are the sons and daughters of God – are unaware of the awesome power at our fingertips. And creation is eagerly waiting in anticipation, on the edge of its seat, longing for the day when Christians will recognise the divine calling placed on their lives and begin to walk with God in creative and redemptive power. The effect will be amazing.

So let me encourage you once again: choose to walk in the authority of the calling that God has placed on your life. Only you and God know what that means. Beware of false humility that is really only pride, focusing as it does on self. Choose to believe what God says instead of being seduced by the enemy's promises of fame and fortune, or frightened by what people will think of you. It's what God thinks of you that counts, and in His eyes you are a precious son or daughter. I pray that you will be one of those sons or daughters of God that creation has longed to be revealed.

Notes

1. Webber, *Worship Is a Verb* (Hendrickson Publishers Inc., 1996).
2. J.A. James, Congregationalist minister, Birmingham 1834, quoted in J.A. Moore (ed.), *Religion in Victorian Britain* (Manchester University Press, 1998) p. 132.
3. Leonard Weaver (compiler), *Gospel Songs of Grace and Glory* (John Bateman, London).
4. K.J. Connor, *The Tabernacle of David* (City Bible Publishing, Oregon, 1976).

5. Mike Bickle, *Growing in the Prophetic* (Charisma House, 1996).
6. The reality is that it's impossible to understand history or current affairs without seeing it as His-story, particularly as God reserves the sovereign right to *'change the times and seasons'* (Daniel 2:21).
7. George MacDonald (1824–1905), *Diary of an Old Soul* (Augsburg, Minneapolis, 1994).
8. Some (including I believe Wesley), teach that perfection is possible, citing, for example, Matthew 5:48 (*'Be perfect as your Heavenly Father is perfect'*), but I'll leave that for others to argue about.

Chapter 6

The Worship Leader

'For long ago, in the days of David and Asaph, there had been directors for the singers and for the songs of praise and thanksgiving to God.'   (Nehemiah 12:46 NIV)

I hope that you're getting excited about worship! In these final days of human history I believe that Jesus is beginning to prepare His Bride to meet Him. We will experience many of the things that our ancestors only saw in dreams and visions – these really are exciting days to be alive. What I've tried to show in the previous chapters is that there is also a challenge in these days to move on from where we're camped – to untie the ropes that bind us to unhelpful human traditions and launch out into deeper, uncharted waters; to become more dependent on Jesus and more heavenly-minded (see Colossians 3:2). I've also tried to show that a renewed emphasis on creativity and vibrant artistic expression is not a recipe for chaos, but that with proper administration we will once again find a voice to express our love-affair with Jesus and that through Spirit-filled prophetic art there will be a two-way conversation with the Creator.

In these next few chapters we will look at how this works out in practice. As a worship leader, administrator or pastor you're probably thinking, 'Help!' It's all very well talking about releasing all of this creative energy, like some kind of spiritual nuclear fission, but how do you manage it? How do we avoid meltdown?

As we've already seen, there are numerous doxological emphases. There is the Quaker approach which tries to minimise overt leadership. At the other extreme there are almost dictatorial models where no one is allowed to breathe without first asking permission. Yet in all situations where Christians meet together as the expression of the body of Christ, there is a need for leadership and order. There are common ingredients: leaders – individuals or groups – responsible before God for what goes on; musicians and other creative people helping to facilitate worship and there is a congregation being led into worship. So let's get practical. In the next chapter we'll look at different ways that worship can be organised and different approaches to leading, but before we do that, let's look at what it takes to be a worship leader.

Philosophy of leadership

Two important principles

If the Church is to grow and function as intended, two things, to quote John Wimber again, are demanded of leaders. These two principles are woven into my own approach to leadership and they form values that help to shape the way we do things. The first is this: leaders must give their churches back to God. The second: leaders must give ministry back to the people.

One dear friend of mine has an international ministry and has been used in amazing ways to touch thousands of people. He has written books, appeared on TV shows, spoken at conferences, and so on. One day, in a hotel somewhere in the States, he felt God speak to him. God, as He often does, asked a question: 'Is this ministry about you, or is it about Me?' It was a question that brought him to a standstill with a sudden shock – a question that ultimately transformed his life and his approach to ministry. So many leaders think in terms of 'my church' or 'my ministry', but unless it's God's ministry we're wasting our time. We need to think of ourselves as stewards rather than owners, managing our affairs on behalf of the Master. Moreover, the time has come to stop working for God, but to work with Him.

In the last few years I have been shocked at the number of leaders that I know who have crashed and burned, disillusioned with this thing called 'church', bitter and negative towards the things of God. There are numerous reasons: Gordon MacDonald called one the 'sink hole syndrome'[1] – the inability to maintain firm personal foundations resulting in eventual collapse; another is the lure of sin, especially in the areas of money and sex; other leaders find themselves constantly criticised from within their own flock – held back from functioning, frustrated; and the fourth reason – the most common that I have seen – is burn-out from having to do everything. I was invited recently to sing at a large church. It was outwardly a very successful church; a well-heeled congregation filed in and took their places facing the front until the building was full. But the poor pastor did everything! He welcomed us at the beginning, dedicated a baby, prayed for a line of people during a ministry time, introduced me *and* preached a sermon. And the people watched the show. The church will remain a spectator sport unless this key issue is faced.

Our role as leaders has to be to mobilise ministry in others. Worship leading is no exception to this. I heard of one church where the organist had been at her post for sixty years! It was applauded as some kind of record, but my response was: how sad! Why had she not raised up someone else to take over her ministry? Right now I am playing in a youth band in our church. I love playing loud music and we have a great team of people. What's more, it feels like we're in the middle of God's flow of blessing. But last week was my last Sunday doing this – it's time to hand on the baton to someone else. In some ways I'm sad, but in others I'm excited to see how God will develop that ministry without me, or rather with me as coach rather than player. So these two principles should be part of our foundation.

Servant leadership

> '... *whoever wants to become great among you must be your servant, and whoever wants to be first must be your slave* ...'
> (Matthew 20:26–27 NIV)

The most poignant and powerful illustration that Jesus gave us about leadership was when He took off His clothes, wrapped a towel around Himself like a slave, and washed the filthy feet of His disciples. It is an image that is burned into Christian consciousness and therefore all the more depressing to see it violated on a daily basis. I've lost count of the meetings I've attended where those on the platform seem more preoccupied with self-promotion or book sales than anything else. And worship leaders are equally guilty, often only singing their own songs so they can get royalties and sell more CDs. As a leader you need to be constantly on your guard against being seduced by the sweet taste of self-promotion, all the more so if your gifts push you on to centre stage.

On the other hand, there is an equally insidious danger of being too self-effacing instead of walking in the calling that God has placed on your life. False humility is just as selfish as pride. Self-effacement and self-promotion are both centred on self. True Christian humility means simply agreeing with God's opinion of you, and if He chooses to promote you to a position of high visibility then do your best to *'walk humbly with your God'* (Micah 6:8).

Character and gifts

Some years ago I was driving with a good friend of mine towards the Harrogate Conference Centre in the north of England. We were due to lead worship together at a conference with a couple of thousand people and I was feeling unprepared. I didn't have any sense of what God wanted me to do, no particular music had come to mind and it was one of those situations where I felt that I was flying blind. I mentioned this to my friend, and he turned to me and said something I'll never forget: 'It doesn't matter what you do, John – it's much more important who you are.' I guess I'd heard things like this before, but at that moment it was as if God had moved it from my head to my heart. I felt the pressure lift from me, and found I could relax – I didn't have to do anything particular, I could just lead people towards God's presence. I understood that God values character more than gifting.

Staying afloat

Let's look at this in another way. The visible part of an iceberg represents only ten percent of its bulk; ninety percent is below the water line. If the ten percent represents gifting, then the ninety percent represents character. Gifts are only surface things; they are the visible, public side of your personality and ministry, yet they cannot function properly without the support of under-lying character, which, on the whole, is invisible. This is why it is necessary to have a secret history with God; that what you do in private supports what you do in public. People that have depth of character are able to stand firm when the wind blows and the waves begin to grow.

I watched a programme once about the life of a superstar musician. The cameras followed him to his holiday hotel (he occupied a complete floor) in which he was installed complete with two rooms dedicated entirely to his wardrobe. During tennis practice on a private court a woman who simply wished him 'good morning' distracted him. He flew into a rage like a petulant child, stamping his foot and screaming abuse at his entourage. He demanded that he be taken back home and within hours, the laborious packing process had begun while he watched and sulked.

When the supporting character begins to dissolve, there is the danger of capsize. Sadly, the musicians' hall of fame contains many who have met an untimely death, sometimes through suicide, sometimes through excessive lifestyles resulting in burnout. All are examples of flawed characters unable to support the weight or expectations of their gifts.

Christians are not immune from this. In my view the problems which 'normal' people face are often compounded by religious complications: false expectations, poor leadership, misunderstandings relating to the role of the arts and, at the extreme, spiritual abuse. The latter results when misguided and manipulative authority figures add a spiritual dimension to behaviour that in itself would be considered abusive. Yet the good news is that God is interested in developing your character. He is a good father. He will take you through situations and expose you to influences that will help to shape and form your inner man or woman. In many ways He is more interested in your character than in your gifts. Your gifts are easy to develop: you can sit in your room for hours on end – as I did as a teenager – refining your guitar prowess, but only God can form real strength of character in you and it's a process which takes time and effort on both sides.

This is particularly frustrating for creative people who are driven to succeed. All you want to do is to exercise your gift to the full, but God works to a different time scale and has more eternal priorities in mind. In my case I spent twelve frustrating years as an electronics engineer and manager. Yes, looking back I wished I'd made some wiser choices, yet God used that time to develop things in my character that I could not have learned any other way. He has a wonderful way to *'make up to you for the years that the swarming locust has eaten'* (Joel 2:25 NASB).

Developing character

Let me give you seven ideas that will help you develop godly character.

▶ *Learn to follow*

My advice to you as someone who wants to develop a ministry is, first of all, to learn to follow someone else. Good leaders are good followers: learn to be a servant. If you have any choice in the matter, look for a coach who will mentor you with godly integrity: someone who's been round the block a few times and has a track record that you can respect. Choose to submit to their authority. If you have no choice, learn to submit to those that God has placed over you. Serve their vision before you serve your own.

▶ *Develop a secret history*

Secondly, develop a secret history with Jesus. This applies not only to private times with him, but relates to how you react to life situations and other people. Soak yourself in God's Word. Jesus taught us to consider others better than ourselves, and to walk in humility. Paul warned us against allowing roots of bitterness to grow up. I am often disturbed at how so many Christians seem to ignore even such basic Christian tenets. So don't just read the Bible, try to live by what you read and fall in love with the writer: remember, it's the menu, not the meal.

▶ *Get connected*

Build relationships with people who will support you but who are not necessarily working with you. Sometimes these will be people from your own locality, but sometimes it's worth seeking out people who have a similar vision to your own or who are involved in similar work from further a field.

▶ *Be accountable*

Find someone (or a group of people) you can be accountable to. This may simply be those God has placed over you in the church, or it could be people from your support group. It is unwise to rely on people under your authority to hold you to account because, more often than not, people will not have the boldness to confront you with issues. So, if you do not have peer relationships with people that will hold you to account, seek them out. But do not do what I've seen some people do, and that's to try and find 'yes men' who will simply flatter them. Choose people that you can trust to challenge you if the need arises. Moreover, since most leadership problems concern abuse of power, money or sex, you need people who have the nerve to be straight with you.

► *Don't be a loner*

Don't be a loner. I believe God designed us to work in teams. If you don't have a team around you then make it a priority to build one. We'll look at many team issues later, but the first step has to be to pray that God will bring the right people to you.

I know many creative people – and I mean many – who live very lonely, introspective lives, and as a result they produce lonely, self-centred art. It reminds me of Elijah who was sucking his thumb one day: *'He sat down under a solitary broom tree and prayed that he might die'* (1 Kings 19:4). Clearly he wasn't having a good day. Elijah's problem was that he was under the impression that he was the last prophet of God left alive. He keeps saying: *'I alone am left, and now they are trying to kill me, too'* (1 Kings 19:10 and 14), so a few verses later God has to gently remind him that there are at least seven thousand other people in Israel who haven't succumbed to worshipping Baal. Maybe this is why Elijah is described in the New Testament as being *'as human as we are'* (James 5:17).

Being connected and accountable, as well as not being a loner, all concerns the need for you to really be part of the body of Christ. So many artists and musicians I come across have limited people skills some could even be described as socially dysfunctional so it's really important to actively seek life-giving, supportive fellowship and learn how to relate to people.

► *Value training*

Get some training. Both in business, but especially in the Church, I find that people are promoted to positions without any training to equip them for the task. Take every opportunity to learn, particularly about skills that are not directly related to your main area of talent. This will help you to become more balanced and effective.

▶ *Know your calling*

The seventh step is to know your calling. I think I have mentioned already that being a leader is, in many ways, like volunteering to be ugly. You will be the target of criticism, people will question your ability and you'll find yourself either put on a pedestal or on a shelf. Furthermore, there will be opposition to your vision – it's not a question of if you have troubles, it's a question of when. It's one of those promises of Jesus that we don't find on the promise calendar in the kitchen. Knowing your calling will help you through the hard times, when the tide seems to be flowing against you. The knowledge that you're doing what God has called you to do will be your anchor.

Although people can help you find your calling, I believe that primarily it results from a conversation between you and Jesus. Somehow you just know that this is what you are called to do. If you struggle with this, think of verses that have had a strong influence on your life, or identify long-term themes that keep surfacing through the years. The likelihood is that these are related to what God is calling you to do. Also, don't discount the obvious things like 'natural' skills. The chances are that when God made you He also gave you gifts for the task ahead. Let me leave you with a verse that has resonated in my life since I was twenty:

> *'Consider now, for the LORD has chosen you to build a temple as a sanctuary. Be strong and do the work.'*
>
> (1 Chronicles 28:10 NIV)

Note
1. Gordon MacDonald, *Ordering Your Private World* (Highland Books, 1986).

Chapter 7

Leading into God's Presence

*Understanding more about the role of
the worship leader*

What are we aiming for?

One day, Jesus entered the Temple in Jerusalem. His step was measured and purposeful as He strode through the dusty crowd of pilgrims. Many were gazing open-mouthed at the building, but He was looking straight ahead, His eyes dark with anger. From outside the city the Temple looked like a jewel sparkling in the distance, the gold dome throwing back the summer sun, but from its cool porticos the towering splendour was over-whelming. The smell of greed hung in the air like a thin veil of pollution and travellers inadvertently clutched their purses as hawkers and street urchins targeted their money. Many had saved for a whole year to make the sacred pilgrimage. To one side, stacked against a smooth dressed sandstone wall, were racks of doves, moaning and fluttering occasionally in the heat of their confinement. Their sweet musty smell made it difficult to breathe. Those who could not afford a lamb for a sacrifice queued patiently in the heat before the desk of the moneychangers, waiting to change their shekels to clean temple currency before joining the dove-sellers queue.

Jesus was incensed. Hastily plaiting a makeshift whip from cords snatched from a nearby stall He strode to the head of the queue. He was not a small man: thirty years of hard labour had given Him the physique of a fighter. Sinews stretched, muscles tensed and eyes narrowed as He approached the stall. He stood there for a moment, His hands slowly tightening on the whip.

The seller did not look up. 'Get to the back of the queue,' he droned, 'you can wait your turn like everyone else.'

Aware of the tension in the air the crowd edged backwards. The stallholder looked up, but it was too late. Jesus struck, and with one angry movement the stall was upended, piles of coins rattled across the courtyard. Before the stallholder could react the whip lashed across his face leaving him moaning on the floor. Yet still Jesus advanced, anger distorting His features. 'This house is supposed to be a house of prayer!' He was almost screaming. 'But you ... ' His toe kicked the cowering form on the ground, 'You've made it a thieves' den!'

With this He turned and smashed into the wicker cages. Soon not one was left in one piece. Frantic birds clawed skywards as a snowstorm of white feathers slowly settled on the broken cages. Jesus stood, breathing heavily. An awkward silence had rippled through the crowd and in the distance someone was shouting for the Temple guards. Ignoring the stares, Jesus turned on His heels, His eyes still smouldering with rage.

Release the doves

As Jesus walked me through this incident, I felt Him speak to my heart about my role as a worship leader. I felt Him say to me: 'John, I want you to release the doves.'

When I stand before a crowd of people as their worship leader I see them often as doves, spirits that were designed to soar on the thermals of heaven. Yet they are caged by religion, by fear, by sin, by pain – some things that are of their own making, others that have been forced on them. But the result is the same: they are unable to fly. So there are two things I must do: firstly, I must break open the cages. Only the Holy Spirit can do this as I work with Him, but what I try and do is get past the religious context. I try to be real and avoid unnecessary religious language and choose songs and music that help to break down, rather than reinforce, the constraints. The gifts of knowledge and wisdom are useful here, as often God will lead me to a particular song that unlocks the hearts of people.

The second task is to invite people to fly with me. This means I need to model worship myself and draw people with me towards intimacy, rather than just telling them that that's what they have to do. I need to hold their hands and lead them towards Jesus.

Build a road

There is another side to worship leading and that is the need to prepare a place where Jesus feels welcome. A.W. Tozer's definition of worship was 'to feel in the heart', and this highlights the fact that worship is a response to the revealed presence of Jesus. You cannot respond to someone who isn't there, so there has to be both an expectation that He's going to come and a preparation so that He feels welcome. You could think of it as a road-building project:

> 'Listen! I hear the voice of someone shouting, "Make a highway for the LORD through the wilderness. Make a straight, smooth road through the desert for our God. Fill the valleys and level the hills. Straighten out the curves and smooth off the rough spots. Then the glory of the LORD will be revealed, and all people will see it together. The LORD has spoken!"' (Isaiah 40:3–5)

This passage is talking about what civil engineers know as 'cut and cover': it means that you cut through the hills and use the waste to fill the valleys, ending up with a level road. Hills and high places speak of the human pride that needs to be removed and valleys speak of those areas where people need a hand up – maybe to be lifted out of depression or sin or other things that prevent them from entering into worship.

Now obviously, as a worship leader, you cannot be held responsible for people's personal worship, but you can help to shape the framework that enables them to draw close to Jesus. As we shall shortly see, your preparation and attitude can have a marked effect. So, sometimes I think of worship as a two-way journey. On the one hand I am preparing a highway so that Jesus can come towards us; on the other hand, I am leading the people with me towards Him. Hopefully, at some stage, they'll meet up! It's then that *'the glory of the LORD will be revealed, and all people will see it together'* (Isaiah 40:5). As we saw when we looked at the passage in Zechariah, this has to be the primary goal of corporate worship. The fact that we seldom experience God's glory does not make it any less biblical or desirable.

What worship leading is not

There is a misconception about worship leading which I need to mention and this is that as a leader you are somehow worshipping on behalf of the people. Whilst analogies with the Old Testament priesthood are useful at times, the role of the worship leader is not, strictly speaking, priestly. The priest's role was to approach God on behalf of the people: your role is to arrange a meeting rather than act as some kind of mediator between God and man: it is not shuttle diplomacy. You are not directly responsible for other people's worship; neither are you a channel through which they offer their worship to God. As Dave Markee points out in his book, this can leave you bearing burdens that you are not supposed to carry and is a common problem among creative people.[1] In some cases it is a contributing factor towards a melancholy, even depressive, spirit.

Different approaches to worship leading

Like you, I've sat through some pretty awful meetings. Well, there's a saying that goes something like this: 'fools learn from experience; wise men learn from other people's mistakes'. So, it is time to gain some wisdom from the mistakes of others. What follows is a bit of a rogue's gallery – a motley collection of worship leaders, all with serious character flaws! What is frightening is that most of them are based on real people, although I am exaggerating somewhat. I don't know how you'll find this, but as I went through these examples of how not to lead worship I realised that I'd behaved like this myself on numerous occasions and it reminded me of one or two incidents that I'd rather hoped had been forgotten! If nothing else, it also shows us that God can use ordinary people like you and me, just trying to do their best. So, don't take it too much to heart – let's see what we can learn.

▶ *The manager*

Many churches struggle with the idea of handing over control of the service to some creative maverick, so instead they appoint someone in a suit whose job it is to oversee the service. This person often sits on the stage, like the headmaster on speech day, sometimes surrounded by lower-grade teachers and departmental heads called 'elders'. In the worst cases, the 'headmaster' is also tone-deaf and can only lead worship by proxy, either by using hand-signals or interrupting with comments and suggestions. Artistic nuances often go straight over his head (or, some whisper, through it) and he is often an accountant or (perish the thought) a theologian or pastor.

Now one of the requirements of corporate worship that we'll explore later is the need to flow. For people to be *'delighting in the LORD's perfections and meditating in his Temple'* (Psalm 27:4), there is a need to avoid unnecessary scene changes or crass interruptions that bring the focus back to the stage. The manager is often insensitive to the aesthetics of worship and would have no idea what Aquinas meant when he described Jesus as 'the art of the omnipotent God'. Often the reasons why churches require strong managerial oversight boil down to issues of control: there is an inherent fear of the unknown, or of releasing others in their calling.

Now, there are situations where this works well, but it does require empathy and mutual respect between the leader and the worship team. I know of one church that takes the Davidic model so literally that the pastor leads the service taking a role analogous to King David, reserving the right to command the musicians to prophecy at a moment's notice (see 1 Chronicles 25:2). It works because there is strong teaching in the church to support their practices, combined with love and respect between the artists and leaders. Where the manager has a good understanding of worship and is gifted to do the job, this can be a very powerful model to use. It has the advantage, when done well, of providing a secure framework within which the musicians and artists can freely function.

▶ *The cheerleader*

This is the most common worship leader I have come across. He tends to bounce out of bed early on Sunday mornings and drives to church in good time, humming songs by a well-known English worship leader. By the time the congregation is filing sleepily into the pews, he is champing at the bit, ready for the off. After a hearty welcome, he likes to encourage the congregation with a brief but uplifting 'thought for the day' before launching into a bone-jarring praise song. He's not too concerned about musical finesse: most songs feature scrubbed acoustic guitar (slightly but annoyingly out of tune), eight scrubs to the bar. He is the eternal optimist and his approach involves much encouragement to 'give God the glory' followed by frequent clap offerings. He tolerates slow, meditative songs, but always plays them slightly too fast as if trying to get them done and dusted as soon as possible. He often works up a sweat when leading, particularly as, like Tigger, he is very fond of bouncing.

Half the congregation love him. Those that don't bounce a little in sympathy during the worship time, forcing a smile but inwardly wincing and glancing frequently at their watches. They pray the prayer expressed in the old hymn: grant us wisdom, grant us courage, for the facing of this hour. And it generally it is a good hour before he allows the pastor onto the stage for the notices.

The problem with the cheerleader is – if we were to be blunt – that he needs to lead worship in order to prove his capability, to find his identity. Underneath he has a heart of gold, which is why he is allowed to continue as a worship leader, but most people wish he could learn to be a little more sensitive when people die or get seriously ill. Unfortunately the church where he leads seldom has time to catch its breath, let alone experience times of intimate communion. Moreover, he finds it very difficult to train and release others for fear of losing his job. The great thing about him is that he is full of genuine enthusiasm and often takes care of jobs in the church that no one else wants to do.

▶ **The DJ**

The DJ is the cheerleader's brother (but attends a different church), so we ought to deal with him next. As his name suggests, his problem is that he loves to talk especially between songs, but any pause in the programme will often do. He often prays extemporary prayers that are shallow, if not trite, using many well-worn clichés. He starts the service by welcoming those that are there for the first time before explaining in not insignificant detail why worship is really important. Before singing the first song, he outlines why this particular song is significant and sometimes feels led to read a scripture that the Lord gave him that morning as he was cleaning his teeth. The song is duly led with a sincerity that is slightly overdone, and although his eyes are closed some of the time, he frequently opens them to check that the congregation are paying attention. At the end of the song he will remind the congregation why they have just finished singing the last song before helpfully explaining why the next song has been chosen. Like his brother, his taste in music is somewhat narrow, tending to go for more up-tempo praise songs most of the time.

Now, there are four main reasons why musicians, or any people who lead worship, talk a lot. The first is that they like the sound of their own voices, enjoying the power of the microphone. The second is that the songs they choose don't really express what is on their hearts, so they then talk to compensate. The third reason is that they are nervous of silence, afraid that maybe something unexpected will happen. More often than not, they are just not comfortable with the concept of intimacy – not only intimacy in worship, but also closeness in human relationships. The fourth reason is a lack of understanding of what worship is really about – of how people need to have space and time to interact with Jesus without constant explanations and interruptions.

The first of these issues is perhaps the most difficult to address as it touches on insecurity and heart issues, but the other three can be dealt with through training and encouragement. With all of these worship leaders we need to recognise that they have a genuine desire to serve, yet need a firm hand if they are to move forward in ministry. You'll be surprised how well they respond if you explain your reasons for wanting to bring correction.

► *The dictator*

The dictator is essentially a control freak. He is a bit like the cheerleader with all the compassion squeezed out of him. He comes in two guises: sometimes as the serious, domineering priest-like figure who seldom smiles yet often stares with rather piercing eyes at the assembled flock; or he wears the mask of super-spirituality – retreating often behind a veil of mystical communion yet making it very clear who is in charge. He has a very supercilious air about him.

The first manifestation often exhibits a breathtaking command of Scripture, but here the Sword of the Spirit is used more to prick the consciences of the worshippers than to edify or encourage. The approach is somewhat cold and cerebral with only an occasional smile to lighten proceedings. Sitting in a service led by him one feels nervous, wondering if he will fix you with his stare or, more worryingly (as I once saw), accuse some of the congregation of failing to worship with sufficient abandon. Whilst he is capable of leading worship – either as a musician or as a 'manager' – he seems almost unable to enjoy worship himself and is unable to relinquish control and allow people to find their own pathway to Jesus. In fact, in his theology he tends to ignore Jesus, preferring instead to address his prayers to Almighty God. He likes hymns with challenging lyrics rather than musical or artistic beauty.

In the second guise, the dictator is equally chilling. He tends to encourage those who view him as someone special, maintaining an aura of mystique and holding the common people (even people in his own worship team) at arm's length. While leading worship, he will often put on a great show of having a direct line to God and, instead of gently leading people into worship with him, he will march boldly ahead expecting them to follow.

The only redeeming features of the dictator are his knowledge of Scripture and his years of experience. The sad thing is that those years have left him with a hard heart and he finds it very difficult to show his true feelings, either for people or for God. He is a hard person to manage and would never be described as a team player. He is often hurting deeply inside and consequently, hides behind a protective shell: if he would only allow Jesus to heal his wounds, the change would be incredible. In fact, I've known Jesus break his heart with a single word, resulting in a powerful marriage of Word and Spirit.

▶   *The transcendental meditator*

The transcendental meditator stands at the front with his eyes firmly closed most of the time. His voice is not very loud, but he's a pretty good (acoustic) guitarist having spent hours in his bedroom working out new chord inversions. Sometimes, when he leads worship, the congregation is unaware that the service has started and they feel a bit guilty when they finally join in on the third song. He loves working in a team, but sometimes the musicians around him get bored. Songs seem to go on forever as he gently sways, gazing (metaphorically) at his navel. He cannot stand 'shallow' praise songs, preferring instead repetitive dirges that lead him towards Nirvana as the congregation dreams of coffee and doughnuts. He likes the sound of the phrase 'deep calls unto deep', but hasn't a clue what is means. He is often quite up and down emotionally: on a good day he smiles gently at people and writes songs, on a bad day he is wracked with guilt and writes songs about the Cross.

The transcendental meditator was given the job because he could do two things well: he could play the guitar and he could model intimate worship. So as far as modelling worship goes, he is well equipped for the job; the problem is that his leadership skills are somewhat lacking. He fails to make eye contact with the congregation at all, so they wonder if he's noticed they're there. Musicians in his team feel the same way. Nevertheless, people will follow him into God's presence because they sense a genuineness that endears them to him.

▶ *The small animal in bright lights*

I know you're going to accuse me of being sexist here, but the small animal in bright lights is a pretty girl. Someone once told her that if she fixed her eyes on a point on the back wall just above the last pew it would look as though she was making eye contact with people without her actually having to look at them. What they failed to tell her was that it's advisable to change the spot occasionally, so now she has a fixed stare that borders on panic like a rabbit caught in the headlights. Her mum says she has a really nice voice, but few people have actually heard it. She's a real sweetie and no one minds that they can't actually hear her sing at all during services except the sound engineer who's gingerly trying to coax sound out of her channel without howls of feedback. When she's feeling really relaxed (and the lights aren't too bright) she closes her eyes and lifts one hand in worship.

Like the transcendental meditator, when the small animal does relax a little she has the ability to draw near to Jesus in worship. People see this and it encourages them to do the same. She doesn't consider herself to be a worship leader, but God does. Although she's a frustrating person to work with (the cheerleader feels like throttling her during rehearsals), with the right training and encouragement she could grow into a powerful leader.

If I was given the opportunity to train and mentor these worship leaders, I still can't quite decide with whom I'd rather work. The dictator is the least attractive, but there's no telling what would happen if he really got fired up (by God, that is). In some ways I'd rather have someone like the cheerleader who is enthusiastic and over-keen: sometimes it's easier to teach someone to cool it a bit rather than having to constantly say 'come on dear, you can do it!' On the other hand I love people who have the sensitivity to woo the dove of the Holy Spirit. Thankfully God can work with all kinds of characters. All of us have the potential to *'be mature and full grown in the Lord, measuring up to the full stature of Christ'* (Ephesians 4:13). If you really identify with one of the above characters my advice is to aim for more balance in your life (and music) by embracing some things that might not come to you as first nature.

The balancing act

Being a worship leader is not easy. There are many dilemmas and tensions. Just the mechanics of coordinating an event involving other musicians and a congregation are daunting: add to that spiritual and emotional dimensions and you have a recipe for ulcers. There is a storm blowing around you. The wind is powerful and, as you spread your wings you feel your body beginning to lift, but at the same time you're trying to dodge bits of debris that are coming at you. You know you need to steer a particular course, yet at the same time you have to be very sensitive to the smallest change in wind direction and take note of others around you. How do you learn to ride the storm?

Freedom and control
Our discussion earlier on the philosophy of leadership raised many issues. In my view, the most important by far is the concept of stewardship. Stewardship embodies the idea of servant leadership because a steward is always accountable to his master. It also underscores the fact that nothing we claim to own is actually ours – we hold all things in trust and one day will have to stand before God and give an account of how we managed our gifts and projects.

A steward, however, that is called to manage a project cannot evade his leadership responsibilities. He cannot function without exercising his God-given authority, but the manner is which he does this is very important. Jesus told us not to lord it over people – to pull rank, if you like – but He never said, 'Don't be a leader.' What we need to understand is the difference between being authoritative and being authoritarian. If you find yourself constantly having to remind people of your position, you're probably being authoritarian. Authority, it is said, is like soap: the more you have to use it, the less you have. Paul certainly did not discourage leadership: he said, *'it is a true saying that if someone wants to be an elder* [Gk. overseer] *he desires an honourable responsibility'* (1 Timothy 3:1).

When leading worship the dilemma is always: how much should I take control of the situation, and how much should I allow 'God' free reign? I put God in scare quotes because this is the nub of the issue: real discernment is needed to know what is God and what is just human enthusiasm. What I'm about to say is really important: I don't think it is possible to make this distinction most of the time. Just as the Kingdom of God is portrayed in terms of yeast spreading through a lump of dough, so the Holy Spirit works in the gathered community of saints. Humanity and divinity are, as it were, intertwined. The sacrifice of praise is not a mystical experience unrelated to the human condition; it is primarily a decision to worship – a choice to lay our lives down on the altar. No more, no less. The role of the leader is therefore analogous to the conductor of an orchestra who uses his artistic interpretive skill to unite the musicians. Yes, there is a mystical dimension as we use our spiritual sensitivity to discern and direct proceedings, but common sense plays an equally important role. Having a good understanding of the issues surrounding worship will get you a long way towards making wise decisions.

My advice is this: if you have been asked to lead worship, don't be afraid to lead. You have not only the right, but also the duty to override contributions from the floor if you deem this appropriate. You must obviously defer to those over you – your senior pastor or leader – but don't be afraid to use your God-given authority. So often I have seen worship hijacked by well-meaning saints: inappropriate confession during a time of intimate adoration; tongues which focus only on the speaker; even horrendous 'prophetic' words which have more to do with the psychological state of the so-called prophet than the Holy Spirit. These things can easily skew a meeting away from the intended focus unless the leader uses a firm hand. The decision is yours, and it underlines the privilege and responsibility that it is to be a worship leader.

We looked earlier at the three sizes of Christian meeting. This helps us to tailor our approach accordingly. What is appropriate for a home group is often entirely inappropriate for a celebration. The following table is a summary.

Festival/Celebration	Synagogue/ Congregation	Home/Cell Group
Inspiration	Identity	Intimacy
Led from the front. High degree of planning and control. No (or rarely) contributions from the floor.	Led from front but more relaxed. More corporate involvement.	Led from within. High degree of flexibility and interaction.

Walking in authority

Most of the creative people I come across do not suffer from over-confidence and if they do this is often a mask for inner insecurity. A heightened sensitivity is both a blessing and a curse. Yes, it results in empathy and the ability to focus on the inner self and the Holy Spirit, but it also results in wounding as people take on board things that they should really let God deal with. You may find yourself fighting a melancholy spirit, feeling swamped by both your own sin and the pain of the world around you. The only way to deal with this is to re-centre your life on Jesus and remind yourself frequently that the burdens of the world are His, not yours.

Isaiah the prophet was told once *to 'shout to Zion from the mountaintops! Shout louder to Jerusalem – do not be afraid. Tell the towns of Judah, "Your God is coming!"'* (Isaiah 40:9). The worship leader must be just as bold. Climbing to the top of a mountain and screaming at the top of your voice demands a certain level of abandonment and a lack of (or choice to ignore) self-consciousness. You need to have the same attitude. Spend less time thinking about what people will think of you and more time performing for the 'audience of One.'

Unlocking your potential

Performance and worship

Now, the word 'performance' is a dirty word in Christian circles, particularly in the area of worship. 'You're not supposed to perform,' we are told, 'you're supposed to be worshipping.'

I was attending a large conference once and really enjoying the worship. The band was amazing, the worship leader was gifted and the sound system was powerful. What's more, I sensed myself being drawn close to Jesus as my spirit soared on the wings of the music. As we worshipped, the leader turned to the saxophonist and signalled for him to do a solo. Here was a man who could play that horn! He had already been playing little figures and fills that danced in the music and, by the rack of expensive instruments, I could tell he was a dedicated player. Well, he began to play and I was immediately brought back down to earth. The dove in me crashed and I found my attention drawn back to the stage. I was puzzled. The solo was lifeless and seemed to dribble out the saxophone onto the floor. The prophetic edge was gone. I knew what had happened. Someone had spoken the curse over him: you're not supposed to perform in worship.

Let me ask you a question: 'How is it possible to play in front of an audience and not perform?' The issue, surely, has nothing to do with performance as such, but more fundamentally to do with whom you are performing for? If you're performing merely to satisfy the needs of your own ego then of course this is not what it's about. I encourage musicians and artists to just go for it: perform to the best of your ability – be as free as a bird! Soar on those wings of worship! Just bear in mind that you are perform-ing for three audiences: primarily for the 'audience of One', but also to serve the audience gathered around you. And it's OK to play for you – there's no rule that says you can't enjoy yourself in worship, is there?

Skill and calling

I once knew a guy who literally knew only three chords and yet (with much use of a capo), could effectively lead people into God's presence. He had a remarkable gift – the ability not only to worship himself but also to bring others with him. I also know artists who do not consider their art very refined, and yet have powerful prophetic ability. So is skill that important, or should we focus more on calling and spiritual maturity?

My daughter Amy drew me an amazing picture once. She was only nine at the time and yet I still have it on display in my study. It's not a very artistic picture: there's a blackbird sitting on top of a hastily-scribbled fir tree, looking not unlike a sausage being toasted above a bonfire. The yellow beak is the give-away. The reason I really love this picture is that Amy chose to depict the time when I was studying a lot, and she and I used to sit together in the garden – her reading her books, and I mine. It was May and the blackbird in the tree spent most of his day singing his heart out. Amy named him Bert and it wasn't long before there was a family of five blackbirds in our garden (all with names beginning with 'b'). The drawing was done for me, and came with the caption: 'To Dad, happy Father's Day, loads of love, Amy.'

You can understand why I love this picture. When I look at it I hear the blackbird sing and I think of Amy and me enjoying the garden together. Isn't this what worship is about? Us bringing our offerings to Jesus that remind Him of our relationship? I don't think He's over-concerned about the quality most of the time. He looks down from heaven and says to God: 'That's my girl down there! Fantastic!'

But what if Amy was still drawing the pictures of a nine-year-old ten years later? As her father I'd be distinctly worried and it makes me wonder what our heavenly Father thinks when He looks down on our art. Many worship leaders I come across are so lazy! They desperately need to mature and invest in their gifts, developing a skill level that allows them to focus less on mechanics and more on worship. We've already touched on the difference between excellence and perfection, so we won't go into that here, but my advice is always to work on improving your skill. Again, it's helpful to think in terms of three types of meeting. I would hesitate before releasing someone to lead worship in larger meetings until they had cut their teeth in smaller settings and demonstrated a skill level appropriate to the task. I'm looking for competence as well as personal integrity:

> *'And David shepherded them with integrity of heart;*
> *with skilful hands he led them.'*   (Psalm 78:72 NIV)

Titles and position

There's one more area we need to consider under this heading and it concerns titles and labels. Now we all like to be given titles like 'Pastor' or 'Managing Director'. It makes us feel valued and helps us with our sense of identity. But titles can also be a curse. Let me give you an example: I once spent time with a musician who had been given the title 'Worship Leader' by his pastor. He was a great musician and a good leader, and yet he came to me almost in a state of depression. 'I'm not a worship leader,' he said, 'just a musician.'

The problem came down to a false expectation of what a worship leader was. He'd been to events where those leading were very exhibitionist in their approach to worship, putting much emphasis on what I would call ecstatic mysticism. I think you know what I mean: a strong emphasis on extroversion combined with high-profile use of spiritual gifts. Because my friend felt he didn't fit into this narrow mould – this narrow definition of 'Worship Leader' – he felt that he wasn't up to the job: a bit like David trying to fit himself into Saul's armour, only to find it more of a hindrance that a help. So titles can be a curse, which is why here in our church we seldom use them. Apart from giving people false expectations, there is also a pride that comes from being called 'Worship Leader'. It is better to focus on function rather than title and position. Don't be afraid to be yourself. You have a unique character and calling and as long as you're not being rebellious God can work with you.

More practical advice for worship leaders

In the next chapter we will deal specifically with team issues, but before we do that we'll look at a few more things that apply more to the way the leader functions.

Get used to hearing God's voice

If you develop a secret history with Jesus you'll soon learn to know His voice, as you would if you spent time with anyone. Jesus Himself promised this, saying that He *'calls his own sheep by name and leads them out'* (John 10:3). Whilst I've tried to de-mystify the mechanics of leading, encouraging you to use your common sense, I do not want to under-value the need to hear from God. I personally have never heard an audible voice, but I have become sensitive to the Holy Spirit's promptings. Often, it's no more than an inner conviction. At times it's the ability to interpret the things going on around you. It's learning what is human debris stirred up by the storm and what is the wind of the Spirit. This process starts away from the stage. As you walk through ordinary life (which, as it happens, is never ordinary!) maintain a conversation with the Holy Spirit and get used to seeing the world through His eyes. You'll be surprised at what you learn.

My advice to leaders is to always be watchful. Eye contact with the congregation is important as it helps to draw people with you as you lead them in worship, but it also enables you to keep an eye on what God is doing. You will begin to recognise certain things as God's activity as He moves among His people. You will then be able to take decisions that encourage the congregation to pursue that path. My example of the guy who started clapping (in Chapter 7) illustrates this: although I simply saw someone beginning to clap in the front row, the Holy Spirit seemed to want me to pursue it further and it resulted in an extraordinary visitation from God. So keep your eyes and ears open as you lead. Listen to that inner voice as well as keeping a watchful eye on the team of people working with you and the congregation in front of you.

Avoid being prescriptive

If you do feel like something particular should happen – say you feel the congregation should kneel before God – my advice is to suggest rather than command. The microphone is a powerful device and is easily abused. Remember that your role is to release the doves, not force them to fly. I've often found that saying something like 'feel free to kneel if you'd like to' is much less threatening or prescriptive than 'let's all kneel now'. You'll find that if it's inappropriate people won't respond; if it is you might like to pursue that path a little further for a while. On the whole, I would advise against being too directorial as you lead; instead focus on providing that environment or framework within which people can make their own choices.

Having said this, there are times when I would cut across what is happening in the room and use my authority to change the direction (or regain control) of the meeting. If, for example, someone in church began to pray out a prayer that I felt was inappropriate, I might choose to ignore him or her and start singing a song. I know it sounds rude, but sometimes you have to be cruel to be kind.

Be gentle and forgiving

Going back to that passage in Isaiah we read a description of God as a good shepherd. It stands out as a prophetic word that tells of the future Good Shepherd. Isaiah prophesies, saying:

> *'He will feed his flock like a shepherd. He will carry the lambs in his arms, holding them close to his heart. He will gently lead the mother sheep with their young.'*   (Isaiah 40:11)

This is a very beautiful picture which reminds us of the feminine side to the character of God. He is concerned to protect and nurture His flock, reminding us of God's words earlier in this chapter where He says: *'Comfort, comfort my people ... speak tenderly to Jerusalem. Tell her that her sad days are gone and that her sins are pardoned'* (Isaiah 40:1–2). I need to say this very clearly: unless you as a leader have a strong understanding and experience of God's forgiveness through Jesus there is a danger that you will abuse the flock. The heart of the gospel is grace and mercy – *'freely you have received, freely give'* (Matthew 10:8 NIV). You can only give away what you have first received. In our churches we desperately need to create a culture of grace and mercy instead of the petty vindictiveness we so often experience. If we don't, we are in great danger of being seriously disciplined by God, receiving judgement without mercy:

> *'Speak and act as those who are going to be judged by the law that gives freedom, because judgment without mercy will be shown to anyone who has not been merciful. Mercy triumphs over judgment!'* (James 2:12–13 NIV)

At times I feel like scolding the flock. Some Sunday mornings, when people are still chatting at the back of the room when the worship starts and no one seems to have prepared him or herself to enter into God's presence, I find myself full of right-eous indignation. On one particular morning like this, leading worship was like stirring porridge. After the first song I was about to make a speech that went something like this: 'Now, come on people! It's Sunday morning! Why are we here? Why don't we take a moment or two just to focus on Jesus before we go any further?' Yet I felt a check in my spirit. Instead, I continued to model worship and encouraged my team to do the same. By the third song there was a real sweetness in the room and the Holy Spirit moved among His children. I was so glad I hadn't told them off. It's so easy to forget what it's like to be an ordinary person in the pew. There is a fine line between making speeches like this and becoming a dictator.

Do what you can to be gentle in the way that you lead and, just as you expect Jesus to know your voice, get to know the voices of your own flock. Good worship leaders are those that have a genuine relationship with the worshippers they claim to lead and are able to provide a secure and loving environment for people to express their hearts to the Good Shepherd.

Expect God's presence

> '... the glory of the LORD will be revealed, and all people will see it together ... Yes, the Sovereign LORD is coming in all his glorious power.'   (Isaiah 40:5–10)

Jesus made it clear that where two or three are gathered in His name, He would be there also. The problem is that we often have preconceived ideas of how God will act. We stereotype and pigeonhole God, only to be disappointed or taken aback when He does something different. I always expected God's presence to be like the glorious power that Isaiah mentions, or like in Chronicles when the cloud of His presence filled the newly dedicated temple (see 2 Chronicles 5). But often it's not like this. All I want to say here is that God will often move in unexpected ways: God's presence does not necessarily mean only 'glorious power'; it could be with a profound sense of peace (see Psalm 131), or even involve a lot of pain (see Psalm 42). It's up to Jesus how He decides to manifest His presence among us; our job must be to lead and pray in the expectation that He will come.

Encourage and release others

As I said before, it's very easy to abuse the power of the microphone, but the problem goes a little deeper than that. Being the centre of attention can become addictive, and selfish leaders love to bask in the limelight, even when leading worship. It can result in people being manipulative: I get really concerned, for example, when people feel they need to lead in order to find their identity. Some will come to you and almost say: 'If you don't release me as a leader I'm going to go totally off the rails because it's what God called me to do,' and such things. This is nonsense and demonstrates only an immature and insecure personality.

As seen, one of the primary roles of a leader is to give ministry back to the people. In practice, this means keeping your eye open for people you need to come alongside in your church and encourage, but during a meeting it also means not selfishly occupying centre stage all the time. You need to keep your eyes open and be alert in case others – especially from your own team – want to contribute. I've sometimes been caught out by someone in my own team who's started a reading or a song while I've been meditating with my eyes closed, oblivious to what's going on around me. I'm not suggesting you never close you eyes, but if as a leader you find yourself worshipping with your eyes closed most of the time, something is wrong.

I often tell my worship team that they are all leaders. If you are in front of a congregation in any capacity then in some measure you are a leader. There's no such thing as 'just a backing singer'. Yes, someone needs to take overall responsibility, but I get very concerned by what I call the 'cult of the worship leader'. We must maintain our focus on Jesus as the honoured guest in worship, and actively involve and promote others.

Don't worry about making mistakes

We'll look at this more in the next chapter, but let me just remind you here that it's okay to make mistakes. It's pretty much impossible to learn a new skill without making a mess of things from time to time, so don't worry when things go horribly wrong. Only a few weeks ago, I was leading a meeting when I decided to do an unrehearsed song with my team. I happened to have some world-class musicians with me at the time but a combination of having a bad chart and having to change the key at the last minute resulted in a performance where the musicians only rarely managed to agree on which chord they were playing. It was so embarrassingly bad that I almost broke down in the middle of the song, crying with laughter. But we carried on to the bitter end with stubborn determination to completely ruin a perfectly acceptable song. It's at times like these you just have to laugh and remind yourself to do better next time!

Involve different art forms

I think that we as leaders also need to cast the net wider and include a wide range of arts in our churches. Think about how you can explore the wonderful creative resources that God has given to you in your church. Think sideways; colour outside the lines! Use the artists, the dancers, the sculptors, and the storytellers. In so much as you are able to, give them both encouragement and permission to get involved.

Release the doves.

Note
1.   Dave Markee, *The Lost Glory* (Sovereign World, Tonbridge, 1999).

Chapter 8

More About Meetings

A practical guide to help you plan and prepare for meetings

'And let us not neglect our meeting together, as some people do, but encourage and warn each other, especially now that the day of his coming back again is drawing near.'

(Hebrews 10:25)

I seem to spend a good deal of my life in meetings – some good, some bad, some most definitely ugly. Some, frankly, seem almost pointless. Yet meetings are a fact of life: not only that, but we are specifically encouraged not to neglect our meeting together. This could be a warning about not bothering to turn up, but it also speaks to us of the need to prepare and administrate meetings properly. We were not designed to be solo Christians: it is in the gathered community of saints that we get food and encouragement and where we give our corporate worship to God. It is where having received strength and encouragement that we find courage to once more go out and live in the hostile environment of the war zone. In fact, one wise old saint once said this to me: 'You know, God doesn't ask us to worship Him because He needs it – as if His insecure ego needed massaging – no, He instituted worship for our benefit because it's as we draw close to Him that we receive His life.' Although this cuts across the idea that we worship simply because He is worthy of our praise, there is much truth in this statement.

We've already covered a lot of ground in terms of how we approach worship leading. Now we need to look closer at the mechanics. Paul once remarked to the Corinthians that: *'it sounds as if more harm than good is done when you meet together'*

(1 Corinthians 11:17). I think you'd agree that our meetings should be life-giving experiences, not strength-sapping ordeals – for both people and leaders. I hope that this chapter will help you towards achieving this.

Preparation

Some years ago I went through a period when I never prepared. It was the fashion to just 'go with the flow' so I would turn up to meetings with very little clue as to what I was doing. This can't be good. In fact I used to get stress dreams where I'd be standing in front of thousands of people who were just staring at me, riveted to the spot, unable to see any song list, desperately trying to work out what to do.

Prepare well but don't be paranoid

So my advice is to prepare well. God can speak to you as you prepare just as easily as when you're on the stage, so don't fall into the trap of equating spontaneity with spirituality. I find preparing a few days in advance is a good thing. If you do it the day before there is always that added pressure which hinders objectivity; it's better to have time to breathe before the event starts. I've found this to be even more necessary if I'm speaking at an event: God will often speak to me between the time I've prepared and the event itself, and these insights are often keys to unlocking the situation.

Remember what we looked at earlier: who you are is more important than what you do. So your preparation is as much about getting right with God than anything else. In fact – now here's a radical thought – I don't think it particularly matters what songs you choose or what programme you put together. If God can speak through heathens and donkeys I don't think He'd have much problem coping in a 'mediocre' worship service. I hope this is taking some of the pressure off you. I think we can get much too hung up on what is the 'right song'.

I was at an event once and it all seemed to be going horribly wrong. The speaker was in mid-flow when he seemed to lose the plot. He eventually sloped off the stage and called on me to sing. I hadn't a clue what to do. I was plugging in my guitar and it began to feel distinctly like one of my stress dreams. My heart was thumping and I was desperately trying to think of the right song. Well, I chose to sing a blues worship song. After about two lines, I was thinking to myself 'wrong choice!' Four minutes later I, like the speaker, sheepishly left the stage and hurriedly found refuge in my chair. The speaker turned to me and said, 'fantastic! Just the right song! Thank you so much!' And I'm thinking: 'Was he really at the same meeting that I was?' This has happened to me so many times that I've lost count. I'll think I've done a terrible job, and people are pumping my hand afterwards saying what wonderful discernment and sensitivity I have. As they're doing this I'm tempted to look cool and think, 'Yes, maybe I have got amazing discernment and sensitivity, it's happened so often it must be true,' but then I remember that God speaks through donkeys.

So, I'll say it again: chill out a bit and don't take yourself too seriously.

Focus on flow rather than themes

You know what it's like on the first driving lesson (before the advent of dual controls): you end up bouncing down the road like a kangaroo desperately trying to get the hang of using a clutch and an accelerator at the same time. Leading a meeting is just like this – you need to know when to accelerate and allow the power to flow, and when to apply the brakes a little. If it's not stretching the analogy too far, you also need sometimes to depress the clutch – to disconnect from immediate involvement and step back to see what to do next.

Flow, for me, is the key. You remember earlier we talked about how people need to lose themselves in worship and gaze on Jesus' beauty. If you're constantly changing gears and turning corners you can end up making the children car-sick. Personally, I've had enough of the stop-start hymn sandwich approach and would much rather provide space for the doves to fly.

Rocks in the stream

To leave cars for a moment and get back into boats, what kind of rocks in the stream to we need to watch out for? What might interrupt the flow in worship? (I'm not talking about unforeseen interruptions here, rather things that you have control over.) Apart from stops and starts, we really need to watch out for anything that focuses attention back onto the stage or, if you like, frightens the dove of the Holy Spirit. Things like:

▶ *Abrupt tempo changes*

By all means change tempo or style when you need to, but this should be a conscious decision. Random changes can be very distracting. Flowing from one song to the next without a too-abrupt scene change is the ideal.

▶ *Unhelpful content changes*

Often people confuse content with style. Fast songs aren't always 'praise' and slow songs aren't always 'adoration'. Try not to jump from confession to praise, then back to confession again before launching into intimate adoration. So think about what the words are saying, not just what the song feels like. Some people advocate various 'flow models', saying, for example, that we should 'enter His courts with praise', and then confess our sins before we go any further, and so on. Usually such models end up in the 'holy of holies' with an intimate song. Personally I find this approach of limited use as the context often demands a different start point, end point or focus, or requires us to linger at a certain point in the journey.

▶ *Talking too much*

Please don't be a DJ – don't plan unnecessary speeches or prayers into your programme unless you have a specific reason for doing so. Of particular concern are random comments and impromptu prayers which, if you take a moment to analyse their content, are just a waste of space and do not help to achieve the goal of flowing in worship.

▶ *Playing badly or out of tune*

Part of your preparation must be to make sure you can play or sing the songs you intend to use for the meeting. This is in the wider context of learning to be a skilled musician. Too many musicians confuse practice with rehearsal. A rehearsal is when you come together to rehearse for a specific goal; practice is what you do in your own time. Both are needed. Learning scales and arpeggios, chords, music theory and so on, is not an option. You need to do this if you aspire to be any kind of public performer. As regards playing or singing in tune: if people are unable to keep their instrument or voice in tune they should not be on the worship team. Exactly what standard you use to measure this is up to you.

▶ *Be as organised as possible*

As you prepare, don't be afraid to be really organised. Some are fearful of organising God out, but if you plan prayerfully you can just as easily organise God in, if you see what I mean. My approach is to plan as best I can but be flexible enough on the day to throw my plan away if need be. The more organised you are with song sheets, overhead slides, stage plans and so on, the more you will be able to relax and hear God's voice.

▶ *Song choice*

When you choose songs, it's good to ask a few simple questions (forgive me if some of these seem really obvious):

1. **Can we play (or sing) it?**
   Is it too complicated for your band to play? Have they actually rehearsed it? Can you play it? If the answer is 'no', you know what to do. Also, bear in mind that a lot of songs written by men are almost impossible for girls to sing comfortably (especially first thing on a Sunday morning!) because they are pitched too high.

2. **What does this song say?**
   Bearing in mind the need for content flow as well as musical flow, understand what the song is about. It's also good to check that it's doctrinally and biblically sound (this applies especially if you are a song writer). Luther remarked once that Christians learn more theology from their songs than from their sermons, so we need to be discerning. In many cases songs are not necessarily wrong, but nevertheless they might not sit comfortably with you. If this is the case, then think twice before you use them.

3. **Do I believe in this song?**
   Continuing this theme, I sometimes ask myself, 'Can I believe in this song?' What I mean is, 'Is this a song I can make my own? Can I sing it with genuine conviction?' Just as you will never lead worship in the same way as someone else, so some songs – great in themselves – might not suit you. Now I know some of you are thinking: 'But surely my job is to please God and help people to worship? If I don't particularly like a song it's hardly a good enough reason for not doing it?' Well it's true that there are times when we

need to lay aside personal preferences and be good servants, but I found it really freeing when I realised I didn't have to like (or use) every Christian song I came across or that was put in front of me. Some songs just create an atmosphere that makes me uncomfortable (some are just horrible), so I don't use them unless specifically asked to. My encouragement to you is to develop your own style, and be as comfortable as you can with the material you use.

4. **Is this song appropriate for the setting?**
Songs which work really well in a celebration are often really difficult to pull off in smaller meetings, particularly if you only have a few musicians and very little in the way of sound equipment. You might also consider time constraints. If there is only time for one or two songs it narrows the choice considerably.

5. **Are there any major issues I need to consider?**
If someone has just died you wouldn't start the service with a loud praise song. Local, national, and international affairs do have a bearing on how we approach God. The sensitive worship leader will take wider issues into account, but may not necessarily allow things to colour the way he or she leads. It's as we worship God that we gain fresh perspective on life, so we need to be careful to maintain that focus and not be too sidetracked by worldly affairs. However, there are times when current affairs will change our approach.

6. **Which song is the key song?**
I've often found when leading worship that one particular song really takes off. Somehow it captures the mood of the meeting. Sometimes it's almost as if Jesus turns up at that point and says: 'Hey, I really like this one!' At other times you can sense an almost imperceptible shift in the spiritual atmosphere – a poignancy and an intimacy as heaven touches earth. What I've noticed is those special moments often coincide with a song that I've felt beforehand would be a key song. So sometimes I ask myself: 'Is there one particular song I feel strongly about today?' If the answer is 'yes', then I try to plan the worship around that song. It becomes a pivotal point. Sometimes I will put it at the end of the worship set and work towards it, at other times I will start the service with this song and move on from there. I've found

this approach to be much more manageable that flow models and themes, and it's amazing how many times this particular song will act as a doorway into the presence of God.

7. **Have I planned for intimacy?**
    Earlier we saw how intimacy with Jesus is at the heart of worship, yet so many meetings seem to come and go without us really interacting with Him. Sometimes we skirt around the holy place, singing songs about how good Jesus is, but never getting close enough to smell His perfume. I like to always give people the opportunity to sing a love-song to Jesus, to embrace Him and whisper words of love. Choose at least one song (or other act of worship) that allows people to do this.

Leading the meeting

How much scope do you have?

As a leader it's a good idea to ask your senior leader or pastor to provide some kind of job description for you. You see, one of the main issues for a worship leader is in knowing how much authority he or she really has – what is his responsibility and what is not. It's difficult to exercise authority without knowing the parameters – you will either make decisions beyond the scope of your role or you'll end up being too hesitant, afraid to be firm and exercise leadership when it's needed. For example, you may feel it's right to change the order of service – maybe put the talk first, or start with communion. You'd need to be pretty clear you were allowed to do this before you went too far in your planning. Or maybe during the service a respected member of the congregation comes to the front with his Bible open, wanting to read something. How do you deal with this? Do you have the authority to override or not? Can you decide who joins the worship team and who doesn't, or do you need to refer this back to the pastor? Clarifying such issues will make it much easier for you to lead.

The stage area

▶ *Choosing where to lead from*

Most leaders automatically place themselves in the middle of the stage, but this may not be the best position to lead from. Apart from the issue of modelling worship which is not man-centred, there are practical reasons why standing in the middle might not be a good idea. For one thing, it's good to be able to communicate easily with your team; if they're all behind you have to do a u-turn to do this. I find standing to one side is best, but wherever you stand, make sure you can see both your team and the congregation. (I remember once leading worship in Liverpool Cathedral from a bridge located about fifty feet up, suspended over the middle of the sanctuary. It was a really bizarre experience!) As leadership involves communication there's no way the worship team can function hidden away behind a pillar or something.

▶ *Tidiness*

Don't forget that churches, like homes, can get untidy. You might get used to it, but for the visitor it's more of a problem. Next time you're responsible for a meeting, think how you'd feel if you were there for the first time. Try and make the stage area as neat as possible: this means cables neatly routed, no papers on the floor, instrument cases tidied away and so on. The same applies to overhead projector slides. In these days of technology there's no excuse for an illegible hand-written mess: use properly printed slides, making sure the author's name and copyright details are clearly visible.

▶ *Psychological barriers*

More often than not there's a big gap between the leaders and the congregation. This does nothing to promote the idea that we're worshipping together. Instead, for the congregation, it can be like watching a show. I guess a lot depends on your overall philosophy of church, but you should at least consider how to bridge this gap. What makes matters worse is that the musicians often hide behind a line of music stands or monitors (or flowers). One thing I suggest to our singers is to keep the music stands as low as possible and turn them sideways – that way they're much less noticeable from the floor.

Recently we've experimented with worship in the round, putting musicians in the centre of the room (facing inwards) with the congregation moving freely around. It's really been fun. One time we also had drummers and percussionists positioned around the perimeter of the room as well so that the worshippers were sandwiched in between. There's no law that I know of which states that we must worship standing in rows.

Leading worship

▶ *Focus on the job in hand*

Do your best to get straight down to the job in hand. By all means welcome people if need be, but try not to spend too much time doing this and definitely avoid long 'thoughts for the day' or long-winded prayers. Bearing in mind the need to make visitors feel welcome, it's also best to avoid jokes or pleasantries that can only be understood if you have inside knowledge. Again, try and put yourself in the shoes of the first-time visitor. Especially near the beginning of the time of worship, you need to be really focused on what you're doing – modelling worship yourself and keeping your eyes and ears open in case God wants to prompt you about something.

▶ *Starting and ending songs*

Some churches have incredible musicians that have rehearsed every detail of a song, including arrangements with slick introductions and endings. Sometimes it's great to do this, but I place more value on the ability to set the scene – to create an atmosphere conducive to worship. Sometimes lingering on a simple rhythm or chord sequence will draw people into God's presence. Try repeating just a simple musical motif, gradually involving other musicians; try maybe singing just one line from a song, slowly drawing the congregation with you. What you need to try and do is get away from the 'show' mentality and instead try to think about how you can involve the people in front of you – how you can get them to begin to express their love to Jesus. Having moments like this where the music can breathe makes for a more reflective atmosphere.

Enjoy Yourself!

Worship leading can have its heavy moments (as when a someone came to the front of a meeting I was once leading and announced he'd had a picture of a severed head – 'and it's this church'!), but most of the time it's fun. Yes, it is a responsibility, but not that big a responsibility. Enjoy yourself! Don't take life too seriously! I'm not suggesting you get flippant, but I have attended too many services that could easily be mistaken for funerals.

John Wimber used to advise us to be 'naturally supernatural'. There's a lot of wisdom in this, because so often we get over-dramatic and intense when God begins to act. We say 'thus saith the Lord' in weighty tones when a simple 'I think God might be saying . . .' would do. Anything you can do to reduce the amount of religious nonsense we have to endure is fine by me.

God can cope

Always remember that God can cope with mistakes. I don't think He's particularly worried when things go pear-shaped as long as we're not being deliberately contrary – in fact I sometimes think the opposite is true. I think He sometimes enjoys making things go horribly wrong so that we don't get too proud. (John Arnott reckons this is one of the primary reasons why God puts people out cold on the floor – it's hard to be proud when you're face down on the carpet.) I've made so many mistakes leading worship that in some ways I don't care any more what people think of me. I've dropped my guitar, nearly fallen off the stage, called out the wrong song numbers, forgotten words (often!), forgotten the offering (a few times), forgotten my guitar (once), laughed (and cried) so much I couldn't lead, refused to play during the collection (because it demeaned my 'art' – really embarrassing), sung 'I must increase and He must decrease', played songs in totally the wrong key, led with my flies undone (now part of the Worship Leader's Three Point Pre-Service Check), sat with the women (in a segregated Swiss service) . . .

I'm beginning to feel a bit of a failure.

In fact, I'm not sure I should be writing this book at all . . .

Chapter 9

Building a Worship Team

'As each part does its own special work, it helps the other parts grow, so that the whole body is healthy and growing and full of love.' (Ephesians 4:16)

Yet another job?

You might be thinking: 'Not more work to do, surely? Leading worship is bad enough without having to build teams as well!' Well, yes, there is more to think about, but this is something which will eventually save you work. Having a good team around you is one of the greatest helps and blessings.

John Donne was right when he said, 'no man is an island': we were designed to connect with others, not inorganically like some kind of machine, but organically – a body that has life and feeling, where each member has a part to play. What I hope to give you here is some practical advice so you don't make the mistakes that I did, for it's in this whole area that Christians especially seem to get it wrong. It's only now after leading worship for some thirty years that I feel I'm beginning to understand some of these issues. I never used to consider myself a leader – I was just a musician that led people in worship – but as time went on I could see that God was teaching me to see myself in a different way. Part of it was a lack of self-confidence common to many creative people, but it was mostly ignorance and selfishness – I hadn't realized the importance of the principle of sowing and reaping. I hadn't realized the need to invest in other people. I wish someone had taught me all of this years ago.

Right now I believe that I should see myself as a 'creative pastor' more than anything else, although as a worship leader you have to wear many different hats at times – music director, sound engineer, writer, arranger, administrator – they're all part of the job. It's not my intention to lay any burdens on you that God didn't intend for you to carry – we've already talked about the burdens that titles can bring with them – all I want to do here is talk from my own experience as a 'creative pastor' and let you decide which areas God wants you to develop.

The word *pastor* is a good one because it means 'shepherd'. Being in the same company as David and Jesus can't be bad. So, from the outset I'd like you to at least consider the possibility that Jesus is calling you to do more than just play music, even if it is worship music – to consider yourself a potential leader on more than just a musical level. Even calling yourself a 'music director' is not enough because, as we've seen, the worship-leading role is inescapably pastoral as the prime goal is to shepherd the flock into God's presence. It becomes even more so when you consider that most of the time you'll end up working in teams. This chapter explores how to be a good team leader and build a strong, healthy team. It's my prayer that some of you reading these pages will be inspired to devote your lives to this amazing calling.

Vision

> *'Suppose one of you wants to build a tower. Will he not first sit down and estimate the cost to see if he has enough money to complete it?'* (Luke 14:28 NIV)

What kind of team project are we talking about? What might it look like? Even more importantly, what might it cost? I suppose it would be good to start with these questions, maybe quickly dealing with the last one first by saying that it could cost you your life. After all, Jesus said that laying down our lives for our friends was a sign of real love. And team building has a lot to do with investing in other people, about laying down your life for others.

But what about the project? Well, I like to think of it as like building a temple, not least because there's reams of advice in both Old and New Testaments about how to build temples, but more because it's one of our main callings as Christians for *'we who believe are carefully joined together, becoming a holy temple for the Lord'* (Ephesians 2:21). So, building a worship team involves putting together a workgroup: a team that will work for the wider goal of facilitating worship in a church. Solomon was a bit overwhelmed when his father David commissioned him to build the Temple, but David's response was:

> *'Be strong and courageous, and do the work. Don't be afraid or discouraged by the size of the task, for the LORD God, my God, is with you. He will not fail you or forsake you. He will see to it that all the work related to the Temple of the LORD is finished correctly. The various divisions of priests and Levites will serve in the Temple of God. Others with skills of every kind will volunteer, and the leaders and the entire nation are at your command.'*
>
> (1 Chronicles 28:20–21)

I believe with all my heart that if you really set your heart on building up worship in your church, God will provide all that you need, and more. It may look daunting, but how can you fail if *'the LORD God ... is with you'*? Moreover, God's promise is that He will provide not only resources, but people. For *'this same God who takes care of me will supply all your needs from his glorious riches, which have been given to us in Christ Jesus'* (Philippians 4:19).

Just one more thought before we go on: you remember we saw earlier how cultural change can sometimes be a slow process? Well, imagine how the ragged band of Israelites felt when faced with the prospect of colonising the then-hostile Promised Land full of idol-worshippers. 'How can we ever get rid of these people?' was their question. God's advice was simple and achievable: *'I will drive them out a little at a time'* (Exodus 23:30). I'm not suggesting that your church is full of hostile idol-worshippers (at least I hope not!): what I'm saying is that you will need to introduce changes, but just take a step at a time under God's direction and you'll do fine.

A vision for your situation

Just as David gave detailed plans to Solomon, so God will speak to you about your situation. Try and use the tools I gave you in Chapter 4 to evaluate where you are now, and then work out some goals for the future. Doing a five-year plan, as I suggested, is a really good idea. If you find it difficult to imagine that far ahead, take time out and visit places where things are developing and learn from them. Not only will you get some good ideas, but you might be able to avoid some mistakes too.

Avoid tunnel vision

God might be calling you to think much bigger than you are now. When Nehemiah and friends began to rebuild the temple after the years of captivity and desolation, Zechariah had a word from God for the king. Now the king's name was Zerubbabel and critics had mocked him for daring to take on such a big task. I imagine him helping with the surveying work, dwarfed against the ruins of the temple, holding up a plumb-line against a broken wall. This is definitely how I feel at times. What is interesting is that he is described as *'a signet ring on my* [the Lord's] *finger'* (Haggai 2:23). In other words, he carried not only the authority of an earthly king, but the authority and seal of God himself. Zechariah's word for him went like this:

> *'Do not despise these small beginnings, for the* Lord *rejoices to see the work begin, to see the plumb line in Zerubbabel's hand.'*
> (Zechariah 4:10)

God rejoices to see the plumb-line in your hand as well, and His words to you are: *'Do not despise these small beginnings.'*

The first steps

How do I start?

Many churches have teams already and one of the big questions is: 'How do I bring change when I already have a team?' Or, 'I've inherited a team from someone one else (and I don't like half the people): what do I do?' Let's just review the first steps you need to take, some of which we looked at in Chapter 4.

▶ **Make sure you have not only responsibility, but also authority**

You have probably been given the job of leading worship without any real explanation of responsibilities or expectations. From the outset, talk with those over you and get a clear understanding of your role. You don't want to overstep your brief. However, now would be a good time to face up to some of the issues we've discussed, especially whether you have the authority to 'hire and fire', and how much is expected of you during meetings.

▶ *After reviewing the situation, make your plans public*
Go through a review process as discussed. Find people you can do this with (they may well be existing team members). Prayerfully ask God for wisdom. Then make it clear what you intend to do. Discuss this with your leaders first. This may be a frustrating time if they don't share your enthusiasm for change, but persevere. Whatever you do, defer to your leaders (or leave the church). Leaders are responsible for the wider vision and your vision must fit in with theirs.

▶ *Make it clear what you expect of team members*
Most teams I've come across especially where volunteers are involved are very vague about expectations. Now would be a good time to put together a job description for team members. Think of things like:

- What time do people have to turn up for meetings – an hour before? Two hours?
- How much are they responsible for setting up?
- How many rehearsals are they supposed to attend per month?
- What is the minimum musical skill level required? How might you define this?
- What is the minimum spiritual maturity required? How might you define this?
- Are there any benefits? (Free CDs? Sponsorship on training courses?)
- Who do they report (moan) to?

This will not only focus your mind as you think through who to have in the team, but it will also give you a tool to evaluate performance and commitment. If you have an existing team involve them, drawing up the job description as much as possible. Agree to use it as a benchmark for future work.

▶ *But I'm working with volunteers!*

Working with volunteers is not so different from working with paid staff. You still need to lead and set clear parameters. It's also a biblical principle for church members to respect those with responsibility for them. What you need to understand is that being a good leader is essentially all about releasing others into effective ministry. Once people realise you're on their side it will be much easier. There will, of course, be conflict but we'll deal with this later.

▶ *Initiate a review period*

Once you have clear working guidelines then get people together and agree a timescale for reviewing the current situation. Over a period of say, three months, spend time discussing team development, worship in the church, the job description and so on. Spend time with the team and with individuals. Agree together that there may need to be changes in terms of line-up and working practices at the end of the period. This will help soften the blow if you have to ask someone to leave (not that you'll be any more popular).

▶ *Don't forget to involve a wide range of artists*

Most worship leaders are musicians and tend to forget about other creative people. Think about how you can increase the creative vocabulary of your community.

How teams work

Team, task and individual

There are three elements to teamwork: you have a team of people, a task that needs to be done and individuals that make up the team. Focusing on any one of these areas at the expense of the others will cause you problems. As a leader you need to feed and nurture all three areas so that the team is healthy and able to do its job. Let's look at these three aspects of team working.

▶ *Team*

A team is a group of people that have come together for a particular purpose. There is a reason it exists, and that is to carry out a task. Moreover, a worship team functions on two levels.

First of all it is a musical ensemble, a performing group whose main task is to lead people in worship; secondly, it's a fellowship group where mutual encouragement, support and ministry take place. As a leader, you need to facilitate team activities that help the team to function in both these roles. These will include rehearsals, meals together, having fun together, praying and ministering to each other and so on. These are activities which help strengthen the sinews that Paul talked about that hold the body together – *'each part does its own special work, it helps the other parts grow, so that the whole body is healthy and growing and full of love'* (Ephesians 4:16). So, there needs to be an investment in the team as a whole in order to build 'team spirit'. Paul gives some very practical advice to the Ephesians to help them work as a team – as a body. He reminds them of their calling, he tells them to be gentle with each other, and encourages them to strive for unity.

> *'Lead a life worthy of your calling, for you have been called by God. Be humble and gentle. Be patient with each other, making allowance for each other's faults because of your love. Always keep yourselves united in the Holy Spirit, and bind yourselves together with peace.'* (Ephesians 4:1–3)

This might be a good verse to put in your job description.

▶ Task

Without a defined task, teams degenerate into little social clubs. Instead of having clear goals to work towards, teams get introspective and become cliques. They forget that there's a world out there and members begin to think that the whole thing simply exists for their benefit. Therefore, the job of the leader is to keep reminding the team of why it exists: to keep an outward focus – reminding people of the vision. This does not mean making little speeches all the time, but it does mean modelling a passion for worship and investing time in things like job descriptions, development plans and visions.

▶ Individual

If you're constantly task-focused nagging people to get the job done, to turn up on time, to keep their music tidy and so on people will begin to feel alienated and under-valued. 'He doesn't really care about me. All he thinks about is his stupid church.' So you need to ask yourself: 'How can I set my people free to be more fulfilled and creative?' Individuals need as much investment as the other two areas. Teams are made up of people who need access to you as leader, care from you as pastor, food from you as teacher, relationship with you as friend and encouragement from you as a mentor. You need to invest in them as people.

Support and challenge

Setting people high-challenge goals without providing adequate support results in feelings of inadequacy and vulnerability – it's the 'small animal in bright lights' syndrome. On the other hand, lots of support without challenge results in frustration and boredom, like passing your driving test and then not being allowed to drive. The following grid illustrates the need to provide both support and challenge.

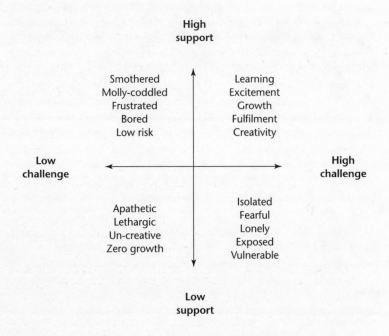

Being a mentor

I've talked about 'investing in people' and 'setting people free to be creative', but how do you actually do this? Apart from giving them permission to do things, how can you develop gifting and calling in others?

The idea of being a mentor or coach is not new. Paul understood this principle because, as an up-and-coming Jewish intellectual, he had sat at the feet of the great rabbi Gamaliel, among others. This is why he advised his followers: *'So I ask you to follow my example and do as I do'* (1 Corinthians 4:16). Paul understood that before he could coach others he needed to have gone through the learning process himself – he himself needed to have developed certain skills before he could pass them on to others. The role of a mentor is also to develop understanding so that people can develop their own gifts in areas that you might never be an expert in. Football managers are not always good players, but they know how to release footballers. You might never be an artist but God might use you to 'release' artists.

The Church is cursed by an intellectual approach to life that results in amazing sermons but little action. This would have been totally foreign to first-century Christians who clearly understood that the goal of teaching was to actually change behaviour, not merely to tickle the intellect. Jesus constantly used a 'theory then practice' approach to coach His disciples: He demonstrated how to cast out demons, and then sent them out to actually do it. So, our approach to developing people must result in concrete action and changed behaviour. This is why I'm trying to be very practical in this book as well as covering philosophy and theology.

The mentoring process

A model that I've found very helpful identifies six steps to effective mentoring:

1. **Identify**
   Identify your disciples – who should be on your team. As a Christian leader you need to be exercising spiritual discernment here, not just practical evaluation. Ask God to speak to you about whom to take on board. You will need to look beyond the surface, considering issues like potential and calling. The obvious people hanging around hoping to be picked for the team may not be the right ones.

2. **Recruit**
   The next step is to recruit them. You will get people nagging you to join the team for all the wrong reasons, but at times

you will have to pursue someone. So many churches have programmes in place, but make it very difficult for new people to join. A recruitment process is part of the doorway into ministry and it needs to be obvious so that people can choose to walk through it if they want to. We'll look more at recruitment in a moment.

3. **Train**

   Often people, particularly worship team members, are simply thrown onto the stage and expected to function. The next step has to be to train people: give them the tools and skill to do the job. You need to make training a priority as you consider long-term (or even short-term) development plans. There is a difference between training and teaching: make sure your training is practical and not just useless theory.

4. **Deployment**

   As seen, Jesus trained people using a 'show and tell' model, followed by deployment. He sent them out to do the job. You may find this difficult because deploying people correctly means that you will have less work to do yourself. You will have to let go of some aspects of 'your' ministry and you may even find that the people you deploy are better at some things than you are. Let's hope so!

5. **Monitor**

   The next step is to monitor progress. Jesus often got the disciples together after a ministry trip for a debrief. 'How did it go? Did it work out OK? What did you learn? Where did it go wrong?' A good coach will watch his team play and then help them learn from their successes and failures. So don't just give people a job and expect them to get on with it.

6. **Nurture**

   I was particularly struck by a comment made by an England football team manager. He remarked that, 'the biggest hindrance to success is the fear of failure'. The Church, of all places, should model tolerance of human weakness, yet instead we are quick to judge, dismissive with our words and heavy with our discipline. As already seen, we desperately need to learn to distinguish between wilfulness and weakness. We need to learn how to *nurture* those in our care. To nurture means to feed, to nourish. It means to provide comfort and support, to encourage and correct. In short – to use Paul's phrase – it means helping the body to *'grow in love'*.

Managing the team

Recruitment

Let's take a closer look at the 'doorway' into the team. You've identified someone you'd like to use, or someone has approached you. Where do you go from here?

► Have a clear recruitment process

I've sat in churches before now, wanting to get involved, but not knowing how to. The first step has to be to advertise: maybe put something in the church notice sheet or mention it at meetings. Whatever you do, it has to be made very clear that you need people; otherwise people will just assume they're not needed (or wanted). I sometimes use a simple application form, which has only two questions on it: 'Why do you want to join the worship team?' and 'What experience/qualifications can you offer?' This tells me a lot about the person! I usually start by giving people the job description so that they know what they're letting themselves in for and what qualifications are expected. But don't write off under-qualified people immediately: always consider offering training.

► Audition

The next step is to audition the person. In most cases I know the person anyway and it's a matter of just getting to know what they can do. It might, though, be worth considering a more formal audition. The added pressure this puts people under does help to reveal how they might cope in a live setting.

► Take your time

Paul's advice to Timothy, *'Do not be hasty in the laying on of hands'* (1 Timothy 5:22 NIV)[1] is appropriate here. It's much harder to 'take hands off' than 'lay hands on' if you see what I mean much harder to close something down than never to start it in the first place. So take your time before you make any kind of decision.

▶ **Recruit for the right reasons**

It's easy to take someone on for the wrong reasons, such as they're there and have been hanging around for a long time wanting to get onto the team or maybe they're a great musician but not really into worship. Or maybe they're a close friend of yours or someone on the team. I sometimes come across people who have been volunteered by someone else who don't really want to get involved at all. The things you do need to consider are gifts, character, compatibility with the team (heavy metal guitarists don't go well with clarinet players) and calling.

▶ **Review period**

If in doubt (or even if not) it's good to say something like: 'Tell you what, why don't you join us for three months and see how you get on? If we decide at the end of that time that it's not working out, will that be okay?' This makes it so much easier to take the hard decision to dismiss someone.

▶ **Qualifications**

We've talked about qualifications at various times, so let me just remind you of the kind of things you're looking for:

1. A servant heart – someone who wants to work with you (and not simply take over your job).
2. Musical (or other) gifts.
3. Spiritual maturity.
4. Availability (no point taking someone on who can never make rehearsals).
5. Demonstrated commitment to the church or project (normally by involvement in a home group or whatever your local indicator might be).
6. A team player.

Use the job description to communicate expectations in each of these areas.

Steve Witt, the pastor from Metro Church, Cleveland, says he's always on the look out for **FAT** people: people that are Faithful, Available and Teachable. But the question is: 'How do you know whether people are like this?' The only way you can know is by having a history with them so, let me say again, take your time before you promote people to positions of responsibility.

Working together

▶ **Communication**

Clear communication short-circuits a lot of potential problems. In these days of email, SMS texting, and mobile phones there's really no excuse for people not to keep in touch. Creative people are sometimes very introspective, so you have to make a bit more of an effort to really connect at times. My advice is to use face-to-face communication for anything that's important, if necessary backing it up in writing. Whilst email and such is very useful, people often hide behind it to avoid real contact, especially when they're not willing to face up to a particular issue.

▶ **Prayer**

I haven't really mentioned prayer much, on the assumption that you're doing this all the time anyway, but don't forget to make this a priority. Each time you come together to lead a meeting you should allow at least a moment (ideally longer) to pray together before you go onto the stage. I try and use this time to specifically lay hands on members of my team and bless them, and to listen out for the prompting of the Holy Spirit. Devote time to prayer away from the stress of leading meetings as well: learn to wait on God together and allow Him to refresh you and give you insight and direction.

▶ **Rehearsing and having fun**

Try and get a balance between formal rehearsals and just having fun together. I am told that the multi-national company 3M requires its employees to account for only 80% of their time on their time sheets – in other words they can 'waste' 20% of their time if they want to. It is significant that some of the most innovative inventions that have made a fortune for the company – like 'post-it notes' – have been thought of in this 'wasted' time. You'll find that leaving space just to have some musical fun will not really be wasted. It's also good to forget the mechanics at times and just learn to 'flow' together in worship and prayer. If you are unable to do this together, how can you expect to lead people into God's presence?

When you do have more formal rehearsals I find it helpful to be as organised as possible. For example, even if people don't read music it's good to use a written part. You should at least have a good idea of the shape of the song and the arrangement, otherwise rehearsals degenerate into a confusing cacophony of good ideas as everyone chips in with their penny worth. Don't be too dictatorial though: great ideas will emerge as you work together, but as a leader you need to learn to be firm when necessary. In particular, take time to rehearse those repeating motifs and rhythms that you can use to draw people into God's presence.

Finally, don't forget to have fun! Go to the cinema or eat out occasionally. I've found that food and musicians generally mix well! Don't forget to involve sound engineers and others that are part of the wider team when it's appropriate.

Dealing with conflict, mistakes and sin

Room to fail

As we saw in Chapter 7, there is a desperate need for the Church to stop being so vindictive and judgmental, and begin to create a culture of grace and mercy. You have the power to make a difference here: as a leader you can give people room to fail. Remember what the football manager said: 'fear of failure is the biggest hindrance to success'. Even if people do sin, correction isn't always necessary – so often we are quick to correct (in love, of course) without asking first: 'Is this really necessary?' My experience is that when I sin I'm only too aware of it – the last thing I need is more condemnation heaped on me by well-meaning guardians of my soul. No. Often gentle encouragement is the best approach to start with. Persistent mistakes or patterns of sin are more serious and it's these things we should be watching out for.

As we approach this subject then, bear in mind that a mistake is not necessarily a sin, neither is conflict per se – conflict is only sinful if driven by sin.

Evaluating a meeting

When we stand up to lead worship, we are making ourselves vulnerable. Although we often pretend to know what we're doing, most of the time we (or I, at least) are acting on hunches and intuitions, steering a tentative course, feeling our way like a blind man following a wall. For this reason I am very slow to criticise others for getting it wrong – one person's 'wrong' is often someone else's 'amazing time'. Moreover, the close of the meeting is most definitely not the time to criticise unless some horrendous sin has taken place.

> *'My dear brothers and sisters, be quick to listen, slow to speak, and slow to get angry.'* (James 1:19)

I suggest the best time for any kind of autopsy (probably the wrong word!) is twenty-four or more hours later. When you do try to evaluate success, focus less on musical performance issues (although these do need to be considered) and more on using your discernment to know whether people were able to worship. Ask questions like: 'Did the people look like they were worshipping?' or, 'Was there too much distraction from the stage?' 'Did it seem to flow?' 'Did God seem to enjoy it?' These are difficult questions to answer because of their subjective nature, but they do need to be asked.

Dealing with conflict

Conflict, I'm sorry to say, will occur. I'd just like to give you a few basic guidelines that will help take the heat out of the situation. Remember that even in conflict our aim should be to build one-another up.

▶ *Three days and it stinks*

Before Jesus raised Lazarus from the dead He told the disciples to roll away the tombstone that sealed the grave. 'But Jesus,' they complained (full of faith), 'he's been dead three days – he'll stink!' So it is with 'issues' between people. The longer you leave them, the more they'll smell. So make it a rule to deal with things quickly if at all possible. It's the same with students and washing up: once it's been there a week or more it needs an awful lot of scraping.

▶ *Don't be too self-righteous*

> *'Most important of all, continue to show deep love for each other, for love covers a multitude of sins.'* (1 Peter 4:8)

Many issues I come across are not really that big a deal, so my advice is to deal with them quickly without you (or the other parties concerned) getting 'super-spiritual' in the process. Let me remind you again that you (and they) need to forgive others just in the same way that you have been forgiven.

▶ *Follow biblical guidelines*

If it becomes a serious issue then it's sometimes wise to involve, for example, your pastor in order to ask his advice. However, don't forget that the first step, according to biblical guidelines, is to try and get the parties concerned to resolve their differences themselves – to meet one-to-one and work things through. Only if this fails to bring resolution should you involve others. I'll leave you to look up the relevant passages (see Matthew 6:14; 18:15 and 5:23).

▶ *Rules of engagement some do's and don'ts*

With the above in mind, we can list a few do's and don'ts relating to conflict management.

Do's

- Do it privately. There is often a hidden agenda in public confrontation coming out of a desire for retribution.
- Do it as soon as possible (remember – 'three days and it stinks').
- Do deal with one problem at a time so as not to confuse the issue and as you do so, be very specific about what you are dealing with and how.
- Do focus on things that can change and make positive suggestions to bring that change about.
- Do affirm the person. You can be sure that the enemy is already trying to undermine the person's confidence, sowing doubt and insecurity. Choose to 'build one-another up in love'.
- Do avoid sarcasm and using words like 'always' and 'never'.
- Do try to understand instead of seeking to be understood. The most obvious thing is to take time to listen.

Don'ts

- Don't walk away from the problem or ignore it (as people often do). See it as an opportunity for growth and deal with it as soon as you can. Artistic people in particular often have a strong desire to avoid confrontation and will do anything to avoid having to face up to something which they find threatening.

- Don't get into a 'winner takes all' situation. Most coins, as you know, have two sides. If possible, resolve the issue so that the parties involved are each left with something positive to take away.

- Don't whine about the problem to everyone else. Apart from being very immature and unbiblical, this will magnify an issue out of all proportion. So often issues that look really problematic are remarkably easy to deal with when analysed objectively.

- Don't get someone else to deal with it. If it's your problem, then obviously you need to deal with it: if it's a problem with others in your team, then act as a broker to get it resolved. Either way, you need to take initiative and responsibility.

- Don't blame someone else. This is often a cover for pride, perfectionism and insecurity. Instead, model humility and take responsibility.

- Don't keep score. Once an issue has been dealt with, try and do what God does – forget it and move on.

- Don't pull rank. Apart from the fact that this goes against the grain of servant leadership, pulling rank indicates a lack of authority. I've said this before: authority is like soap – the more you use, the less you have.

- Don't make a truce. This is essentially just an avoidance technique. Like weeds in the lawn, you can be sure that the issue will surface before too long in some form or another until the root is cut out.

- Don't apologise for confrontation; instead, see it as an opportunity for growth.

Colouring outside the lines

I've used the term 'setting people free to be creative'. Let's think how this applies to working together in a team. For a moment we need to think again about what it means to be creative. You may find the conclusion surprising.

Crossing boundaries

When we talk of creativity, we use phrases like 'pushing the boundaries' or 'colouring outside the lines'. By nature, the creative process involves doing new things – you can't create something that already exists. So, creative people in your team will be restless for new experiences and new ways to express those experiences – they will get bored quickly with religious routine.

Creativity is also experimental: often we don't really know where we're heading and what the final outcome might be, but it's fun trying. Creativity, like worship, is a journey into the unknown, whose destination is not sure. Here, in Manchester, we've recently organised worship evenings and given people real freedom to experiment. We've created artistic space such as graffiti walls and art exhibitions; we've encouraged musical experimentation with mass drumming and string quartets; we've used story telling, poetry and prose; we've used our bodies as dynamic mass sculptures. As we've done this, I've encouraged people to 'push the boat out', to genuinely try something new.

Setting boundaries

At the same time we need boundaries. I've talked about providing a framework within which people can worship. Frameworks have boundaries – or do they? Churches certainly have boundaries: behavioural lines which we are not allowed to cross, some sociological, some coming out of the oral law that we discussed earlier – conventions generally accepted to be the norm. But by far the most common boundaries are biblical – or at least we claim they are. Yet it Chapter 3 we saw how the various streams within Christianity have interpreted biblical truth with such multi-coloured diversity that it is difficult to say that only one is 'right'. The jewel that is Christianity has many sparkling faces that reflect the glory of the Creator. Is it possible for us just to say that boundaries must be 'biblical' (would you, like Saul, be allowed to prophesy naked in your church)?[2]

Certainly in recent years I've experienced things in worship that I would have thought entirely wrong only a few years ago and yet, when you step back and analyse things, most of the 'wrongness' is due to pride, preconceptions and cultural conditioning more than anything else. This is going to sound really simplistic, but I would like to suggest that there is only one boundary that we Christians cross at our peril and that is the boundary into sin.

As a leader, you do need to give guidelines to people, but my approach is to talk more about values and principles than fixed lines that people should not cross. If there are specific things that you do not want people to do (like, for example, spend too much time talking between songs) then you need to make that clear. If people cross that line deliberately with a defiant attitude, then that is sin because the Bible makes it clear that leaders are supposed to lead and what they say must be respected. Think of it like bringing up children: you raise them to respect certain rules that must be obeyed (or else!). At the same time however, you want them to be fulfilled as people, having the freedom to experiment, to find their own way in life and be creative. Beware then, of being too petty in your approach. Create an atmosphere where people feel free to experiment, and where mistakes are allowed. Be a good daddy to your kids.

Releasing prisoners

Many of God's creative children are locked in their rooms. Some are still waiting for someone to tell them about salvation, some once fell in love with Jesus but then found that they couldn't cope with the sterility of His Church. Many, like Roy Buchanan – the son of a Baptist minister and one of the world's greatest blues players – took their own lives in desperation. And yet the primary goal of Jesus' life and ministry was to release prisoners. His mission statement was:

> '... to preach Good News to the poor ... to proclaim that captives will be released, that the blind will see, that the downtrodden will be freed from their oppressors, and that the time of the Lord's favour has come.' (Luke 4:18–19)

This passage refers back to the principle of Jubilee – that every fiftieth year land would be restored to the original owner, debts would be forgiven and slaves would be set free (see Leviticus 25). The mission to free prisoners is so central to the Christian message that it cannot (or should not) be ignored, and yet how many prisoners are still waiting for us to act? How many blind people are still waiting for us to give them sight? I suggest to you that we need to seriously consider how to release the creative prisoners around us.

Historically, scholars say that the Jubilee year was never observed. Somehow the Israelites could never bring themselves to let go of those things they called their own – it was just too much to give back land, ignore debts and release valuable slaves. In the same way, I feel that art and creativity has never really been released in the Church. Yes, we've had our renaissances and moments of glory, but our culture is still waiting for those sons and daughters of God to be revealed. We're still waiting for God to restore the missing jewel of worship that A.W. Tozer talked about.

I believe it is the year of the Lord's favour. And so I feel a deep yearning for the Church to become a safe, creative space – to make it a place where artists once again feel welcome instead of having to go out and prostitute themselves in bars, clubs and theatres. Where leaders genuinely lead with a servant heart, wanting to release others into their gifts and calling. Where Jesus is worshipped with such creative passion that even the fabric of our culture changes. This is the call on our lives. I hope that future historians will not look back at us and say: 'They never had the courage to do it.'

Notes
1. Some translations say, *'don't be too hasty in appointing an elder.'*
2. See 1 Samuel 19:24.

Chapter 10

Riding the Storm

'I watched the old man close the door
And turn his back upon the storm
I lift my hands up to the sky –
I embrace the wind.'

You've been very patient with me as we've dug down into the roots of worship or looked at the practicalities of building a team. I hope, though, that you also felt a thrill run though you as we looked at the multi-coloured extravagance of creative, artistic worship. Yet in many ways we're still earth-bound, if you see what I mean – our feet still in the clay of humanity. At times, maybe most of the time, we are fearful, and afraid to spread our wings. Because yes, we do have wings: mine have been folded for most of my life, but now they grow stronger with each passing day and I long for the day when I will have the confidence to laugh and spin in the thermals of the storm.

But right now I'm a little nervous. The overcast sky smells of thunder and there is certain heaviness in the air. I feel it sometimes, almost as a weight on my shoulders. Indeed, unless I'm much mistaken, I feel the first few drops of heavy rain scything into the dry ground and in the distance I hear a faint murmur of thunder, or is it the beat of angel wings?

The storm

For most of my life I've felt a little bit like Elijah's servant, running out to scan the horizon, his hand shielding his eyes, watching for the tell-tell signs of the coming rains. But, like an

African child, I've often been disappointed. And yet it seems that hope has been stirring in me for many years and as I look back (as I encouraged you to do occasionally) it's as though God has been preparing me for these days. I share this story with you, because I know that I was not called to fly alone.

In the mid-eighties I was working as a production engineer near Cambridge. Travels, at least for the moment, seemed at an end. I was out of public ministry apart from leading worship here and there and doing the occasional concert. At the time it seemed like a bit of a backwater – I knew I was called to be a musician, perhaps even a prophet, yet here I was stuck in a boring job. Yet God in His graciousness used this time to teach me many things which have served me well, one of which was to bring a particular verse to my attention from Hebrews:

> *'Once again I will shake not only the earth but the heavens also.'*
> (Hebrews 12:26)

This verse resonated through me. It got under my skin and wouldn't go away.

In 1980s Britain, 'Thatcherism' ruled and a culture of 'every man for himself' developed, which still scars our society. Although recession seemed to lurk close by, the god of materialism was definitely enjoying the limelight. In those days of prosperity, God seemed to keep saying to me that a storm was coming. I scanned the horizon but still saw nothing.

Radical worship

Later that decade, the weather forecaster Michael Fish infamously calmed our fears about the approaching 'hurricane' predicted by the French Met Office. He was wrong. One hundred mile-an-hour winds hit the south of England, uprooting trees and causing structural damage. It was during a walk in the woods on the appropriately named Gog and Magog Hills near Cambridge that God spoke to me again. Surrounded by fallen trees, some of which had stood for centuries, I was heartbroken at the pointless devastation. As I stared around me in disbelief it was as if God said: 'Only those trees with deep root systems will survive the storms.'

This is a simple and obvious truth, yet very profound. In Psalm 1 the righteous man is portrayed as a tree planted by the riverbank, its deep roots reaching into rich soil, prospering and bearing fruit. This is contrasted with wicked people who *'are like worthless chaff, scattered by the wind'* (Psalm 1:4). Like the house built on sand, it is washed away by the storm. I thought to myself: 'I want to be strong enough to withstand the wind. I want to be radical in the true sense of the word.' But then I thought: 'What if the wind is God's power? Do I want to just withstand God's wind, or do I want to embrace it?' In the back of my mind I was thinking of the trees that *'clap their hands'* (Isaiah 55:12) in praise to God. It prompted the 'Song of the Tree', which had the lines:

> 'I watched the old man close the door
> And turn his back upon the storm
> I lift my hands up to the sky –
> I embrace the wind.'

The 'old man' was a picture of religious fear; an unwillingness to embrace the wind of change with the resulting mess that it would cause in the house. So, instead of equating the storm with God's judgment on the world, I felt it applied to judgment on us as His Church. In my heart I knew that there was something of the 'old man' in me – someone who would prefer the comfort of earthly routine rather than heavenly uncertainty. And yet I longed to have the bravery and freedom to lift my hands when the storm came, but I knew that I would need deep roots.

It is for this reason that we must develop a secret history with Jesus. Remember, the root system of a tree is often bigger than the visible part. If we, in this new millennium, are genuinely serious about embracing the wind of the Spirit we have to be rooted. It means we must re-discover the Word of God so that we're not like tumbleweeds – *'blown here and there by every wind of teaching'* (Ephesians 4:14 NIV). It also means we must re-focus on Jesus, the Rock, instead of all the surface rubbish that typifies so much worship and clutters up the house. So many times in history the Church has been derailed by the more subjective aspects of spirituality that characterise prophetic gifts and ecstatic mysticism and it is ironic that the very means that God uses to bring immediacy and life to encrusted religion is the same thing that can bring heresy and death. Yet without the storm, the Church grows weak and complacent. The only solution is for us to have secure and healthy roots – to be radical. So my prayer for you is this:

> *'May your roots go down deep into the soil of God's marvellous love. And may you have the power to understand, as all God's people should, how wide, how long, how high, and how deep his love really is.'*   (Ephesians 3:17–18)

The story is not over. In fact this was really only the beginning, but before we end our journey together I need to expand a little more on the concept of 'prophetic worship'.

Prophetic worship

Prophecy

To *prophesy*, as we have seen, literally means to 'tell forth' in the sense of revealing the things of God that might otherwise be hidden. It is often used in the sense of telling the future, but Christian prophecy is not only predictive, it concerns revealing God's 'mind', past, present or future. The Bible is the ultimate prophetic book because it reveals God's master plan and His heart, although there are many other things that could be described as 'prophetic'. The Creation, as we have seen, is one, as is a good sermon when God's Word is accurately expounded. You are also, as we shall shortly see, prophetic.

Paul's description of prophecy, however, suggests immediacy to the revelation, a direct line to God in order to know His will for a particular situation. Paul would have been familiar with false prophets, such as the renowned Delphic Oracle, or those associated with the first century 'mystery religions' and yet he still encourages us to prophesy, and it's not half-hearted: Paul tells the Corinthians to *'also desire the special abilities the Spirit gives, especially the gift of prophecy'* (1 Corinthians 14:1). Knowing the pitfalls, he takes time to give practical advice, but never discourages us from being prophetic.

The purpose of prophecy

I remember being invited once to the house of a man who was known internationally as a prophet. I felt like confessing all my secret sins before I got there, just in case he *really* knew what he was doing! To my surprise he was a remarkably down-to-earth kind of guy – strange at times, but certainly nothing to be afraid of. There was a confidence about him that was striking, but this was balanced by obvious humility and gentleness. I found myself riveted to what he was saying and came away feeling much encouraged. I realise now that when the prophetic gift is functioning properly it should always be like this, not striking fear into people, which is a common caricature. The 'prime directive' for the prophetic ministry is found in 1 Corinthians:

> *'But one who prophesies is helping others grow in the Lord, encouraging and comforting them.'*   (1 Corinthians 14:3)

We see here that prophecy should result in growth (edification), encouragement, and comfort. This gives us a good starting point when trying to discern whether God is in the prophetic words or songs that people bring: weird and negative stuff has probably more to do with the prophet's own fallen character than God.

Levels of the prophetic

Paul links prophecy to faith. This is not just any old faith, but a faith in the risen Lord Jesus, again illustrating the need to be well rooted. He also implies levels of prophecy – the more faith you have, the more you should prophesy (see Romans 12:6). Some have suggested three levels. In each case let's look at how it might apply to worship.

► *Everyone is prophetic*

It was through the Holy Spirit working in you that you became a Christian and, as a result, you've become a visual aid to others of God's grace and mercy. You shine for Jesus because you have His treasure inside your *'earthen vessel'* (2 Corinthians 4:7 KJV). The writer to the Hebrews says: *'For everyone, from the least to the greatest, will already know me'* (Hebrews 8:11). So in a very real sense every single Christian is prophetic: this is why John writes in Revelation that *'the essence of prophecy is to give a clear witness for Jesus'* (Revelations 19:10).

The clear message here is that *'where two or three gather together because they are mine, I am there among them'* (Matthew 18:20). We don't have to work ourselves up into some kind of ecstasy or trance to be prophetic, or even exercise spiritual gifts as such.

Simple worship offered in faith by believers is music to the ears of heaven, and God and His angels will stoop to listen, however humble the offering. It is prophetic.

▶ *The gift of prophecy*

The next level we come across is the gift of prophecy. Rather than considering spiritual gifts as things that you own, think of them rather as tools that the Holy Spirit will give to you for specific situations, as the need arises. Some people may use this gift more often than others, but it doesn't necessarily make them 'a prophet'.

The Greek word for 'gift' is *charisma* which literally means 'grace gift' which, going back to your Sunday school days, means that it is part of 'God's riches at Christ's expense' for you. It has nothing to do with how many Brownie points you've earned: you can't do anything to earn a gift – it's a gift! Paul says that God *'has given each one of us a special gift according to the generosity of Christ'* (Ephesians 4:7) and yet so often I see Christians proudly strutting around thinking, 'I've got a gift and you haven't!' Yes, we need to exercise faith in order to use the gifts we are given, but don't think of the gift itself as some kind of merit badge. As Mike Bickle puts it: the Holy Spirit gives His gifts to you in order that you become the gift to the Church. This leads him to the significant conclusion that:

> 'If we understood that the manifestations of the Spirit are for the common good, and not for the good of the individual whom God uses, we would be less likely to stumble over the idea that God uses imperfect, often immature people to bless the church.'[1]

When we meet together, those with prophetic gifts are the eyes and ears of the congregation. Not only do they see and hear, but also they 'tell forth' – God speaks through them as we *'declare the praises of him who called* [us] *out of darkness into his wonderful light'* (1 Peter 2:9 NIV). In a sense, the role of the prophet is to make people aware of the light, and as the light is revealed we should expect to see more clearly.

Being creative and being prophetic are, in my view, almost synonymous. The nature of creativity, we noted, was to bring into the light the things that were previously hidden in the imagination of the artist: the prophet is simply carrying out the same process under the direction of the Holy Spirit. When Moses said, *'I wish that all the LORD's people were prophets and that the LORD would put his Spirit on them!'* (Numbers 11:29), he was probably writing with his worship leader's hat on because having such creative/prophetic people on your worship team is an incredible asset. Ask God to show you who those people are.

▶ *The office of prophet*

For some people, the prophetic gift is so strong and consistent in their lives that it would be right to call them prophets. It is their calling, just as some are called to be teachers or evangelists (see 1 Corinthians 12:28). When we think of prophets we tend to immediately think of the Old Testament, but remember that Jesus Himself was known as a prophet (see Matthew 11:19; 21:26) as was John the Baptist (see Matthew 13:57; 21:11). We also come across *'a prophet named Agabus'* (see Acts 21:10) who predicted a famine and warned Paul not to travel to Rome (see Acts 11:28) and also Philip's *'four unmarried daughters who had the gift of prophecy'* (Acts 21:9) – it's not just a job for the boys.

As with any high-profile office in the church, more accountability would be demanded of a prophet than someone who merely uses the gift occasionally. One would look for a strong and godly character as a key qualification and it would be right to judge words with more rigour and respect.

In the context of worship I sometimes come across people who are clearly prophets in that the use of the prophetic gift is more than occasional. Instead, it seems to be intertwined with their creative gift in a special way. The songs that they write or the art that they create seems to be consistently and powerfully prophetic. Some have high-profile ministries and their art has the depth and power to affect nations. As a team leader, you need real wisdom to pastor such people (especially in cases of strong gifts and low maturity) because people often assume that highly gifted people are called to lead as well. This may not be the case. (Bickle's book explores these issues in detail from a pastor's point of view.)

It saddens me when I see musicians and artists who have given up on the church (or have been rejected by the church) clearly exercising prophetic gifts in a secular environment. You can almost hear the Devil laughing at our inability to incorporate

prophetic arts into our churches. Unless we get our act together
the trend will continue. Songs from hell are twisting truth in our
nation simply because we've washed our hands of the responsibility of pastoring the prophetic. Damien Hirst, whose art is
disturbing to say the least, is an example of this. He says:

> 'I always think that art, God and love are really connected.
> I've already said I don't believe in God. At all. I don't want
> to believe in God. But I suddenly realized [sic] that my
> belief in art is really . . . similar to believing in God. And I'm
> having difficulties believing in art without believing in
> God. And it's, like, if I don't believe in God, I can't believe
> in art.'[2]

How many other lost prophets are out there waiting for the
Church to tell them about the reality of Jesus and give them a
place of refuge?

Prophetic worship
So what might the term 'prophetic worship' mean? A definition
might be: 'worship that consciously reveals or declares God's
glory and is a response to His revealed presence'. The opposite, as
we saw in the opening paragraphs of this book, is religious worship that smells of death. Rather than shutting down prophetic
gifting, it is worship that values prophetic people and the gift
they bring to the church.

Not just words
Prophetic symbols and acts are well known, but what is less
obvious is how God often uses instruments or art to prophesy.
Prophetic pictures are common and it's often as we dig into the
symbolism that the meaning is revealed. Think, for example, of
Jeremiah's almond blossom: at first all he saw was a branch of a
tree, but as he explored the imagery (and word-play) the meaning became clear (see Jeremiah 1:11–12). Physical art can be just
as prophetic. It may be surprising but instrumental music can
also prophesy. I've known people to suddenly start weeping
during my guitar solos, not because the playing was *that* bad but
because the Holy Spirit was using the notes to call out to their
hearts, just as He intercedes for us in a way that *'cannot be
expressed in words'* (Romans 8:26).

Practising the prophetic

John Wimber's encouragement to us to be 'naturally super-natural' is wise advice. God is mysterious enough without us adding a little human mystery of our own. God wants to communicate with His children so we shouldn't make it even harder for Him by being obtuse in our approach or suddenly start speaking in King James English. Let's face it, some Christians are just weird most of the time and it has nothing to do with God!

As the exercise of spiritual gifts is very subjective we need, as we've seen, to be firmly rooted. This speaks of being biblically rooted and focused on Jesus, but it also speaks of being rooted in the body of Christ. We don't allow just anyone to minister in our church – however spectacularly gifted they are – no, we look first for character and accountability which can only come through having a history with that person or through reliable recommendation. It is through having a shared life together. However dramatic the gift, you need to be sure of someone before you hand them the microphone. The numbers of creative people that minister regularly in the church here in the UK that have apparently no accountability is rather worrying. They are promoted and given a platform merely because they have a dramatic, visible gift or a charismatic character. They claim to be part of the church but in reality have no connection with the body; like the arms of people with cerebral palsy, they flail about often causing much damage because there is a faulty connection to the central nervous system.

With these things in mind, I will suggest some guidelines for releasing people in their prophetic gifts, because that's what it amounts to – releasing. If you as a leader do not release – give permission and support – then either it won't happen, or you'll suddenly have an explosion of 'gifting' which comes more from human frustration than from God. Either that or your creative, prophetic people will simply leave and find somewhere (not always a church) where they can function.

▶ *Start small*

The beginning of a tree develops underground. The seed takes root and begins to grow. In the same way, the prophetic gift grows as you interact with the Holy Spirit in daily life. Sooner or later, though, your gift needs to see the light of day if it is to bless the church. You'll eventually need to stick your neck out and take the risk to be prophetic. It's a vulnerable position to be in. For this reason, start small. Practice in your home group, your worship team, or with friends. Learn from your mistakes and have the humility to accept correction. Like a trainee tightrope walker, start with the wire pretty close to the ground, with plenty of cushions (people you can trust) around you.

Seedlings are often planted inside protective tubes that keep out predators and provide additional strength during the early years of growth. The important thing as you start out is to make sure that you have the covering and protection of caring people around you. So many prophets (indeed Christians) never make it to maturity because they get terminally damaged early on in the growth process, or they grow twisted by scar tissue that permanently disfigures their ministry.

▶ *Sing songs to God, not songs from God*

Don't put yourself under unnecessary pressure by claiming to be God's mouthpiece. It takes discernment and experience to develop the ability to hear the gentle voice of the Holy Sprit and, even when you are pretty sure that He has revealed something to you, it needs to be delivered with humility. So in the first instance, try singing a new song to the Lord – develop the ability just to flow in praise.

▶ *Soak up God's Word*

> *'Let the words of Christ, in all their richness, live in your hearts and make you wise. Use his words to teach and counsel each other. Sing psalms and hymns and spiritual songs to God with thankful hearts.'*   (Colossians 3:16)

It's interesting that Paul's council to *'let the words of Christ ... live in your hearts'* precedes his command to *'sing psalms and spiritual songs'*. It's as though he's underlining the fact that worship is a response to the revealed word of God. A good chicken tikka masala (now apparently England's favourite meal) is prepared by soaking the chicken pieces in a rich marinade before cooking the meal. The result is a beautiful flavour that permeates the whole dish. In the same way, the more you soak up the words of Jesus, the more your worship will be Christ-flavoured. As Jesus commented: *'Whatever is in your heart determines what you say'* (Luke 6:45, and also Matthew 12:34).

▶ *Prophetic worship is not necessarily spontaneous*

I warned earlier against the dangers of equating spirituality with spontaneity. It's a common mistake. There's no law which says you can't prepare a prophetic song in advance, is there? Similarly, taking an existing song written by someone else can be just as prophetic as an ecstatic outpouring of praise. Its effectiveness as a prophetic act (which 'tells forth' the things of God) is determined by timing and content only, not by who made it up and when. I even went so far as using a Christine McVie (Fleetwood Mac) song in a service once. It ruffled a few feathers, but I felt that in the context it spoke volumes about God's love.

▶ *Use a safety net*

Sooner of later you will progress to the high wire. Just as you wouldn't launch out a hundred feet above the audience in the big top as a complete novice without the use of a safety net, so you need to prepare a net to catch you when you make prophetic mistakes. The main strength in the net comes from a well-articulated theology of failure. Additional support comes from having a team of 'catchers' around you.

▶ *Make room for the prophetic in your programme*

It's so easy to put together a slick programme that organises God out. Try and think of ways to organise God in. One way is to allow space instead of frantically jumping from one item to the next. Allow times for those lingering moments when the Holy Spirit comes like a dove and rests on us.

▶ *Don't overdo it*

Paul's advice that *'let two or three prophesy, and let the others evaluate what is said'* (1 Corinthians 14:29), was given to counter increasing chaos in Corinthian services. There is a real danger that the over-use of spontaneous songs and prophetic words will leave people bewildered and confused. This is particularly true in larger meetings where most, if not all, of the prophetic contributions are coming from the stage. It can very easily degenerate into a spectator sport or, as I've often seen, the congregation feels let down and left behind, as if the musicians are going off somewhere and couldn't care less if the congregation is following or not. Remember the need to draw people with you into God's presence; this demands a certain amount of discipline in providing musical (or other) contributions that are easy to join in with.

▶   *Remember the 'prime directive'*

Prophetic words are rarely directive or correctional, but instead the focus should be on edification, encouragement and comfort. Likewise, prophetic songs or other artistic contributions should focus primarily on encouraging people to enter in to worship. Prophetic music, art, movement and song should all be offered with this in mind. Because of the mystical nature of the prophetic gift there is a tendency, as we've noted, for people to be weird with it. The tone of voice goes falsely authoritative or mysterious; the vocabulary changes; song lyrics become more and more difficult to unravel. Try and encourage people to stay normal (hard for some, I know), and remind them that: *'Since you are so eager to have spiritual gifts, ask God for those that will be of real help to the whole church'* (1 Corinthians 14:12).

▶   *Let love be your highest goal*

The motivation to be prophetic is often fuelled by anything but love (except perhaps the love of showing off). I've seen people basking in attention like spoilt kids, abusing the flock with words of discouragement, wounding people because they themselves are wounded. So we really do need to *'let love be your highest goal'* (1 Corinthians 14:1). Love should drive us and motivate us in the same way that it motivated Jesus, eventually leading Him to the point of laying down His life for us. Love really does cover a multitude of sins.

Flying high

Storm warning

It was a clear, warm evening with a beautiful deep blue sky fading fast towards night. I was seated in the Red Rocks amphitheatre high in the Rocky Mountains, west of Denver, Colorado. As the sun set, the city glowed orange in the distance. At first only a few stars could be seen, but within half an hour the sky was dusted with sparkling starlight. Bonnie Raitt was on the stage and, as the clapping from the previous song died away, the band eased into a slow ballad about a relationship on the verge of collapse. The words pierced my heart and to my surprise, I found myself crying:

> 'Storm warning
> Feels like a heavy rain
> Wind's on the coast tonight
> We may get tossed tonight . . . '

I don't normally get emotional at concerts. Yes, the band was amazing and Bonnie's delivery was full of heart-rending emotion, but why was I crying? It was the Holy Spirit trying to get my attention. I knew this because a year or so before we had had an extraordinary visit from God in our church and during that time I had spent many hours doing what is euphemistically known as 'carpet time', crying my eyes out. Part of it was God dealing with old wounds, but as time went on I realised that it was also a prophetic empathy – that in some strange way the Holy Spirit was crying through me. Often I would cry for no apparent reason (I thought for a while that I was going crazy), but then understood that it usually related to a particular thing that the Holy Sprit wanted to bring to my attention. One striking instance of this was when I walked into a church that had the phrase from James – *'mercy triumphs over judgement'*– written on the lintel of the doorway. As I walked through that doorway I broke down as the Holy Spirit suddenly burned that truth into me.

Soon the band had moved on to foot-stomping R&B, but I was left with a storm warning in my heart, knowing that God was up to something.

The storm of the Lord

A few years later, God gave me what I would describe as a night vision – a very vivid dream that changed my thinking on worship. I dreamt that I was staying with some other people in a house that I took to be Swiss. It had an internal balcony and lots of exposed woodwork (I later came across it in North Carolina). I dreamt that I went to bed and then had a dream within a dream that was extremely vivid and dramatic.

I found myself standing in the centre of a straight, country road. I took it to be American prairie country – a vast plain stretching as far as the eye could see, covered in wheat. The first thing that struck me was the brightness of the sunshine; the wheat was white instead of yellow, like an over-exposed film. As I watched, I saw people running towards me, some to my right, and some to my left, fearful and running past me as if trying to escape from something. I looked up towards the horizon and saw what I took to be a vast, black tidal wave coming towards me, but as I stared I saw that it was a storm. Clouds boiled and lightning flashed in the distance. It was rolling steadily towards me but it was so far away it appeared almost stationary. I remember thinking to myself: 'Wow! That thing must be four miles high!' It spanned the horizon from left to right and, as I watched the people trying to escape, it struck me how futile it was to try and out-run it. Once again I found myself saying: 'It's pointless trying to escape from that! This is the big one!' With that I 'woke' and found myself back in the wooden cabin and announced to those who were with me: 'I've just seen the storm of the Lord!!!!!' I then really woke up and lay there pondering what all this meant. Some weeks later I was reading Isaiah when a remarkable passage caught my eye. It said this:

> *'The moon will be as bright as the sun, and the sun will be seven times brighter – like the light of seven days! So it will be when the LORD begins to heal his people and cure the wounds he gave them. Look! The LORD is coming from far away, burning with anger, surrounded by a thick, rising smoke. His lips are filled with fury; his words consume like fire.'*   (Isaiah 30:26–27)

Instantly, my dream came to mind. I continued to read. The chapter is mainly about judgement: God lays into His people for not running to Him for help, chastises them for putting their trust in human effort (see Isaiah 30:1–15). However, always you sense that He has a father's desire for reconciliation – He wants to bless them:

> *'But the LORD still waits for you to come to him so he can show you his love and compassion.'*   (Isaiah 30:18)

The anger of God then turns to the surrounding nations who have capitalised on Israel's weakness. He threatens to *'pour out like a flood on his enemies, sweeping them all away'* and *'sift out the proud nations ... and lead them off to their destruction'* (Isaiah 30:28). But then God addresses Israel again, prophesying a strange scenario:

> *'But the people of God will sing a song of joy, like the songs at the holy festivals. You will be filled with joy, as when a flutist leads a group of pilgrims to Jerusalem – the mountain of the LORD – to the Rock of Israel. And the LORD will make his majestic voice heard. With angry indignation he will bring down his mighty arm on his enemies. It will descend with devouring flames, with cloudbursts, thunderstorms, and huge hailstones, bringing their destruction.'*
> (Isaiah 30:29–30)

This was an image of worship I had never experienced before – of joyous worship accompanying the judgmental wrath of God. What's more, the imagery becomes very graphic:

> *'And as the LORD strikes* [his enemies], *his people will keep time with the music of tambourines and harps.'*   (Isaiah 30:32)

This is not worship for wimps!

No use running

I have thought long and hard about these images over the last three years. The picture of the storm still burns in the back of my mind, like the image of a bright light burned into my retina. God is still showing me things through this image, but some things are clear. The first is this: there's no point trying to hide or run away from the storm.

The people in my dream are symbolic of those who are trying to escape from God. This concerns two types of people: those who are trying to simply ignore God – rebellious sinners, and also those who are trying to run from God's call on their lives, who *'weave a web of plans that are not from my Spirit'* (Isaiah 30:1). In particular, I want to speak to those of you who know you are called to lead radical, Spirit-filled worship but are running from your calling. There may be many reasons why you are running – maybe one concerns wounds you've already received trying to follow God – but I believe that in these critical days in the life of this planet you may be one of those 'sons and daughters of God' that creation and the Church are longing to be revealed. The time has come to stand up and be counted, to choose to run back to God and embrace His will for your life *for 'the LORD still waits for you to come to him so he can show you his love and compassion'* (Isaiah 30:18).

Spread your wings

> *'But those who wait on the LORD will find new strength. They will fly high on wings like eagles.'*   (Isaiah 40:31)

Being a tree that is firmly rooted is a wonderful analogy of stability and security. You will be able to laugh at the storms that come your way, especially if you are one of those trees that is *'planted in the house of the Lord'* (Psalm 92:13 NIV). And yet for some there is a higher calling and this is to spread your wings and fly on the wings of the wind. I believe God is looking for those who will choose to embrace the wind and rise up on the thermals of His love, having the sight and insight of prophetic eagles.

> I believe the storm of the Lord is coming and there will be some structural damage. I have no doubt that our Western ways will be challenged as never before, but I am becoming more convinced that it also means some damage to the house of God – at least to those parts of the house that are merely man-made structures. The choice is yours: to try and run from your calling, or to turn and face the wind of the Spirit and ride the storm.

Notes
1. Mike Bickle, *Growing in the Prophetic* (Charisma House, 1996).
2. Damien Hirst and Gordon Burn, *On the Way to Work* (Faber and Faber), p. 86 and p. 88.

If you have enjoyed this book and would like to help us to send a copy of it and many other titles to needy pastors in the **Third World**, please write for further information or send your gift to:

Sovereign World Trust
PO Box 777, Tonbridge
Kent TN11 0ZS
United Kingdom

or to the **'Sovereign World'** distributor in your country.

Visit our website at **www.sovereign-world.org**
for a full range of Sovereign World books.